Eternity

Eternity

KNOWING YOUR PLACE IN GOD'S FOREVER PLAN

CHARLES R. SWINDOLL

with study helps by Val Harvey

BROADMAN PRESS
NASHVILLE, TENNESSEE

© 1986 by Charles R. Swindoll, Inc.

Originally published by Multnomah Press

Portland, Oregon 97266

Study questions © 1993 by Broadman Press

4261-36

ISBN: 0-8054-6136-1

Dewey Decimal Classification: 236

Subject Heading: ESCHATOLOGY

Printed in the United States of America

This volume is affectionately
dedicated to four faithful men:

Cyril Barber

Bill Butterworth

David Lien

Bill Watkins

----

who serve behind the scenes at Insight
for Living, giving counsel and
encouragement to those who hurt,
finding in Scripture the foundation of
their faith. I am indebted to each man
for his unswerving commitment to
God's truth, his unselfish ministry to
people in need, his unceasing
discipline to stay at an endless task,
and his unsurpassed loyalty to my wife
and me as friends.

Contents

Introduction 9

Part I: Heaven and Hell 19

  1. Visiting the Real Twilight Zone 21

  2. Resurrection: Promises and Procedure 28

  3. Destiny: Hell or Heaven 35

  4. Preparation: Response and Result 42

  5. An Interview with One from Beyond 46

  6. Biblical Hope for Christians to Claim 53

  7. Ultimate Realities for Non-Christians to Face 57

  8. Major Questions Worth Answering 63

Part II: The Return of Christ 71

  9. His Coming Is Sure . . . Are You? 73

10. Extremes that Block Our Balance 77

11. Predictions that Affirm Our Assurance 83

12. Scriptures that Describe Our Destiny 91

13. Actions that Reveal Our Readiness 99

14. Until He Returns . . . What? 103

15. The Appointed Time 108

16. But . . . in the Meantime 114

Notes 128

Introduction

For years I have wanted to write on doctrine . . . Bible doctrine. My flesh has been willing, but my spirit has been weak. That calls for an explanation.

The need for knowledge of the Scripture is obvious. Everywhere I turn I meet or hear about well-meaning Christians who are long on zeal but short on facts . . . lots of enthusiasm and motivation but foggy when it comes to scriptural truth.

They have a deep and genuine desire to be used by God, to reach the lost, to serve in the church, to invest their energies in "the kingdom of God and His righteousness," but their doctrinal foundation is shifting sand rather than solid rock. The result is predictable: They are at the mercy of their emotions, flying high one day and scraping the bottom the next. A frustrating yo-yo syndrome.

I know. For more years than I care to remember, I, too, climbed and tumbled, soared, and submerged, thought I knew the scoop, then later discovered how off-target I really was. The whole miserable mess leaves a person filled with doubt and disillusionment, grossly lacking in confidence, not to mention having that awful feeling of being exposed. At that point, most Christians decide to pack it in lest they get caught again in a similar position of vulnerability. You and I may be amazed to know how many have retreated into the background scenery of passivity simply because their ignorance of the basic building blocks caused them embarrassment.

Like I said, the need is obvious. Being a fixer-upper type, I am prompted to jump in with both feet and crank out a pile of pages that will provide the doctrinal ammunition so many Christians need. That's why I said my flesh is willing. But since I am also a let's-be-realistic type, I am reluctant. Among the last things believers need is another dull volume on doctrine. Sterile and unapplied theology interests no one living in the real world. Most of those books wind up as great (and expensive!) doorstops. They also make a good impression when the pastor drops by for a visit and sees them lying there, freshly dusted, on the coffee table. And there is nothing like wading through thick theological works late at night to cure your battle with insomnia. Who hasn't come close to fracturing his nose on an eight-pound volume while trying to make it past page 3 in the prone position?

That's why my spirit is weak. Deep within me has been this growing fear of just pumping out another thick, boring book on doctrine that looks good but reads bad.

Theology Needs to Be Interesting

Since I am committed to accuracy, clarity, and practicality, I loathe the thought of publishing something that is anything but interesting, easily understood, creative—and yes, even captivating. See why my desire to write a book on doctrine has been on the back burner so long? It isn't easy to communicate the deepest truths of the Bible in an interesting manner. It has taken years for me to be convinced that it can be done . . . and even more years to be convinced that I may be able to do it. The chapters that follow are my best effort at accomplishing this objective. Only time will tell whether I have achieved my desire.

If my stuff makes sense, if the average individual is able to follow my thinking, picture the scenes, grasp my logic, come to similar conclusions, and later pass on a few of those thoughts to someone else, then the book will have made the impact I desired. But if it lacks real substance, or if the reader discovers it requires a graduate degree to track my thoughts, or even if it proves to be true to the biblical text yet comes across as tedious and pedantic, then my face, I can assure you, will be as red as your nose.

Introduction

The Need to Improve Theology's Reputation

Frankly, theology has gotten a bum rap. Just ask around. Make up a few questions and try them on for size in your church. You'll see. Many folks, if they are candid with you, will confess a distaste for sound biblical doctrines. Sound theology, like Rodney Dangerfield, "don't get no respect." You question that? Then let me suggest you do your own personal survey among some Christians. Ask things like:

- Ever made a study of the doctrines in the Bible?
- How would you respond if your pastor announced plans to bring a series of pulpit messages on several "important theological subjects"?
- Do you believe that all Christians ought to know where they stand doctrinally, or is that more the business of the clergy?
- When you hear the word *theology*, do you have a mental image of something interesting and stimulating? Or do you honestly think, *Dull stuff . . . please don't bore me?*
- On a scale of one to ten (ten being most important), how high would you rate a knowledge of theology?
- Can you remember a doctrinal sermon—or one lesson on theology you were involved in—that you actually *enjoyed*?
- Choosing your preference, rearrange these topics in the order you consider most interesting and timely. Which interests you the most? The least? Give each a number from one to seven.

    _____ a biographical look at a biblical character

    _____ a verse-by-verse analysis of a book in the New Testament

    _____ a serious study of biblical doctrines

    _____ what God's Word teaches about the home and family

    _____ moral, social, and ethical issues according to Scripture

    _____ biblical principles for success and personal motivation

    _____ Proverbs made practical for today

Unless you are most unusual, the study of doctrine would be ranked toward the bottom, if not altogether in last place. Compared to success principles on the home and family, "a serious study of biblical doctrines" does not seem nearly as important or relevant to most evangelical congregations. Yet, believe it or not, at the very heart of all those other topics is a great deal of theology.

It is surprising for most Christians to hear that their doctrinal position determines their interpretation and application of Scripture—whether or not they have ever declared themselves doctrinally. What roots are to a tree, the doctrines are to the Christian. From them we draw our emotional stability, our mental food for growth, as well as our spiritual energy and perspective on life itself. By returning to our roots, we determine precisely where we stand. We equip ourselves for living the life God designed for us to live.

Why Is Doctrine Often So Dull?

If all this is true, then why does the mere mention of theology turn off so many people? Why are most churches full of people programmed to think that doctrine is a synonym for dullness and boredom?

At the risk of appearing ultracritical, I'll be frank with you. Much of the problem lies with theologians who have done a poor job of communicating their subject. No offense, theological scholars, but you are notorious for talking only to yourselves. The language you employ is clergy code-talk, woefully lacking in relevance and reality. The terms you use are in-house jargon, seldom broken down into manageable units for people who aren't clued in. You may be accurate and certainly sincere, but your world is like the television series of yesteryear, "One Step Beyond." Please understand that we love you and respect you. No one would dare to question your brilliance. We need your gifts in the body and we admire your ability to stay at the disciplines of your studies. We just don't understand you.

As a result, much of what you write is kept within those cloistered chambers that intimidate people who haven't had the privilege of probing the heavenlies as you have. The majority feel a distance from you when you share your secrets. I realize that many of you wish this weren't so, but I suppose it comes with the territory.

In this book and the others in this study series, my hope is to build a bridge of theological understanding with the common man, the uninitiated individual, the person who has never been to seminary—and doesn't care to to go—but really does want to develop a solid network of doctrinal roots.

I'm interested in reaching the truck driver, the athlete, the waitress, the high school student, the person in the military service, the homemaker who has a houseful of kids at her feet, the business person whose world is practical, earthy, tough, and relentless . . . and a hundred other "types" who have the brains to absorb biblical truth but lack the time and patience to look up every sixth or seventh word in a dictionary.

I therefore make no apology for approaching various subjects in a different way than standard theologians. I want everyone who picks up this book to understand every word and grasp every principle, even if you don't agree with them. (To disagree with me is your privilege—I expect it. In fact, I invite it. But to misunderstand or to *fail* to understand what I'm getting at would be tragic.)

I freely confess that I want you to enjoy this journey . . . to find out that discovering doctrine and seeing its importance can encourage you like nothing else. I want us to laugh together, as well as think together, as we dig into *the Book*. It's been my observation for the past twenty-five years of ministry that there is no subject too deep for anyone to understand if the material is presented creatively and clearly, sparked periodically by humor, and accompanied by illustrations that let plenty of life in. All this is true of folks who really want to learn.

By the way, that brings up another reason doctrine is dull to some people. As I implied earlier, they have a built-in, long-standing *prejudice* against it. Somehow, they have convinced themselves that (a) they don't need to fuss around with heady stuff like that since they aren't doing "full-time ministry," or (b) even if they made a study of the doctrines, all that knowledge would be of little practical value. In subtle ways these two excuses tend to plug their ears and clog the learning process.

Without trying to perform an overkill, both of those excuses are totally erroneous. Because every Christian is "doing full-time ministry," being theologically informed and equipped could not be more important. And since when does a knowledge of important facts lack practical value? If I recall Jesus' words correctly, that which makes us free is knowing the truth. It's ignorance that binds us, not knowledge. Furthermore, we are left defenseless before the cults and other persuasive false teachers if we lack this solid network of doctrinal roots. As I stated earlier, it stabilizes us.

An Approach that Will Keep Things Interesting

Before we get underway, let me explain my plan of approach.

I have no intention of writing an exhaustive theological treatment on all the biblical doctrines. (If you happen to be a perfectionist, expecting every jot and tittle to be addressed in this volume or the others in this series, please read that sentence again.) My plan is to offer a broad-brush approach to most of the essential points of evangelical truth. If you find certain details are not covered to your satisfaction or if you observe that some subjects of interest to you are not even mentioned, just remember that is on purpose. I'm hoping to whet your appetite for a much more intense and thorough study *on your own* once you've begun to get excited about these essential areas. Who knows? Maybe one day *you'll* be the one who will write a more thorough and analytical work. Be my guest.

You'll also want to keep a Bible handy. I'll try to quote as many of the main verses and passages as possible. But there will be times that I will give an additional reference or two which you might want to look up right then. If you have the time, please do that. Before too long you will begin to feel much more at home in the Scriptures. And use a good study Bible rather than a loose paraphrase or a copy of just the New Testament.

There are a number of study tools that make the Bible and its people come to life for you. *Commentaries* explore books of the Bible and tell you what scholars have discovered about the writers of the books, the times in which they lived, and what the Scriptures mean. *Bible encyclopedias, dictionaries,* and *handbooks* contain information about the people, places, and events in the Bible. They often include drawings and pictures to help you put yourself in the first-century world. *Bible atlases* have maps that show how the Holy Land looked at various times throughout history. Atlases usually give background information about governments and geography. *Concordances* tell you where words appear in the Bible. Pick a word like *love;* look it up just like you would in a dictionary; and you'll find a list of verses in which *love* is used. If you're serious about Bible study, you'll want to stop by a bookstore and invest in a good Bible handbook, atlas, and concordance. You'll be surprised how much those resources will add to your study.

At the end of the first chapter of each part of this book you will note several thoughts I call "Root Issues." These are simply practical suggestions designed to help you keep the doctrines out of the realm of sterile theory and in touch with the real world. To get the most out of these, I'd recommend that you purchase a handy-sized spiral notebook—your personal "Root Issues Notebook"—to record your thoughts, observations, and responses. Each chapter concludes with study questions. "Extending Your Roots" helps you explore what we've been talking about. "Taproot" takes you even further in your study of each doctrine. Don't be afraid to write your answers in this book. It's yours—make it personal.

Ten Major Areas of Doctrine

Finally, the outline I want to follow will be interwoven in this series of five study guides. All the doctrines I want to cover will fall within these ten major categories:

- The Bible
- God the Father
- The Lord Jesus Christ
- The Holy Spirit
- The Depravity of Humanity

- Salvation
- The Return of Christ
- Resurrection
- The Body of Christ
- The Family of God

As I mentioned earlier, the list is purposely not exhaustive, but there is plenty here to get our roots firmly in place. In fact, the better-known historic creeds down through the ages have included these ten areas. While considering this recently, I decided to write my own doctrinal credo, a statement of my personal faith. What it may lack in theological sophistication I have tried to make up for in practical terminology.

As I return to the roots of my faith, I am encouraged to find the time-honored foundations firmly intact:

- I affirm my confidence in God's inerrant Word. I treasure its truths and I respect its reproofs.
- I acknowledge the Creator-God as my Heavenly Father, infinitely perfect, and intimately acquainted with all my ways.
- I claim Jesus Christ as my Lord—very God who came in human flesh—the object of my worship and the subject of my praise.
- I recognize the Holy Spirit as the third member of the Godhead, incessantly at work convicting, convincing, and comforting.
- I confess that Adam's fall into sin left humanity without the hope of heaven apart from a new birth, made possible by the Savior's death and bodily resurrection.
- I believe the offer of salvation is God's love-gift to all. Those who accept it by faith, apart from works, become new creatures in Christ.

- I anticipate my Lord's promised return, which could occur at any moment.
- I am convinced that all who have died will be brought back from beyond—believers to everlasting communion with God and unbelievers to everlasting separation from God.
- I know the Lord is continuing to enlarge His family, the universal body of Christ, over which He rules as Head.
- I am grateful to be a part of a local church which exists to proclaim God's truth, to administer the ordinances, to stimulate growth toward maturity, and to bring glory to God.

With confidence and joy, I declare this to be a statement of the essentials of my faith.

That's where I stand . . . sort of a preview of coming attractions. Now it's time for you to dig in and discover where you stand. With God's help I think you will find this study one of the most important and interesting projects you have ever undertaken. You may even get so "fanatical" about your faith that your whole perspective on life changes.

Come to think of it, that's exactly what Christianity is supposed to do . . . change our lives.

I wish to thank my long-term, splendid secretary as I have so many times before. Helen Peters has done it again. Without regard for her own needs and preferences, she has deciphered my hand scratching, typed and retyped my manuscript, verified my footnotes, corrected my spelling, and helped me meet my deadlines. "Thank you" seems hardly sufficient to declare the depth of my gratitude. I also want to thank Val Harvey for her excellent work in writing the study questions for each of the volumes in this series.

And now let's dig in. You have stumbled your way through shifting sand long enough. May these books on Bible doctrine give you just the help you need so that you can stand firmly and finally on a foundation that is solid as rock.

Charles R. Swindoll
Fullerton, California

Part

I

Heaven
and
Hell

1 | Visiting the Real Twilight Zone

The crisp voice of the late Rod Serling is still familiar to many of us. Those well-enunciated words. That inimitable style. And always such a creative script to carry the audience from the world of the seen to the unseen, out of the realm of the now into another dimension called "The Twilight Zone."

Serling, the original host of that television series, was a master at grabbing our attention. And those haunting strains of music . . . only four notes, but oh, so captivating! The series is enjoying a renewal of interest these days, which is understandable.

"The Twilight Zone" programs never fail to take us into another world where the bizarre appears real—where the things we fear become the very things someone else faces. Interestingly, it isn't uncommon for the stories to deal with death and life outside the here and now. One of the reasons for that, perhaps, is that most people are fascinated by that subject. And the fascination is growing. There is even a name for the subject—*thanatology,* from the Greek *thanatos,* meaning "death." Thanatology is the study of death.

Thanatologist Edwin Shneidman, for example, found that the first time he taught a course on death at Harvard, two hundred undergraduates from Harvard and Radcliffe showed up in a classroom that could seat only twenty. Since then, colleges everywhere have been offering courses, seminars, and dialogues on death and dying. Topics like grief, immortality, suicide, euthanasia, and out-of-body experiences are extremely popular on both high school and university campuses. There seems to be a renewed interest, certainly in our time, in after-life phenomena, especially in visions. Even the medical profession, once suspicious of such things, is now sitting up and taking notice.

J. Kerby Anderson, a research associate with Probe Ministries and lecturer on college campuses, finds his classes packed out. He has revealed in his book, *Life, Death, and Beyond,* "Students are signing up in order to try to register for my course later in the year." Yes, there is a growing interest in the *real* twilight zone.

Death: Its Inevitability and Effect

You and I are going to die. There is no escaping it. Who hasn't heard of the two inescapable facts: death and taxes. I like the comment one wag made: "Maybe death and taxes are inevitable, but death doesn't get worse every time Congress meets."[1]

Arnold Toynbee, the philosopher and historian, insightfully wrote:

> Man alone . . . has foreknowledge of his coming death . . . and, possessing this foreknowledge, has a chance, if he chooses to take it, of pondering over the strangeness of his destiny. . . . [He] has at least a possibility of coping with it, since he is endowed with the capacity to think about it in advance and . . . to face it and to deal with it in some way that is worthy of human dignity.[2]

For the next few pages I want us to do those things that Toynbee suggests. I want us to think about it in advance. I want us to face it head-on. That means that rather than denying it, we shall come to terms with it. Death is sure, and just because we will no longer be seen on earth is no reason to believe that we'll stop existing. On the contrary, that which is invisible may be just as real as that which is seen and heard. Maybe more so!

Sometimes death is sudden. Sometimes it is long and

drawn out. Occasionally, it's beautiful, sweet, and peaceful. At other times it is wrenching and hideous, bloody and ugly. Sometimes it comes too early, which we call "premature." On other occasions it seems the cold fingers of death linger too long as some dear soul beyond the age of a hundred endures in pain and sadness, loneliness, and even loss of mind. But it come, there's no getting around it.

What Does Scripture Teach?

Scripture speaks often and clearly about death. Here are just a few samples from God's Word:

You will have to work hard and sweat to make the soil produce anything, until you go back to the soil from which you were formed. You were made from soil, and you will become soil again (Gen. 3:19, GNB).

Who can live and never die? How can man keep himself from the grave? (Ps. 89:48, GNB).

Seventy years are given us! And some may even live to eighty. But even the best of these years are often emptiness and pain; soon they disappear, and we are gone (Ps. 90:10, TLB).

There is a right time for everything: A time to be born, A time to die; A time to plant; A time to harvest (Eccl. 3:1-2, TLB).

The person who sins will die (Ezek. 18:20).

Sin came into the world through one man, and his sin brought death with it. As a result, death has spread to the whole human race because everyone has sinned (Rom. 5:12, GNB).

For just as all people die because of their union with Adam, in the same way all will be raised to life because of their union with Christ (1 Cor. 15:22, GNB).

Everyone must die once, and after that be judged by God (Heb. 9:27, GNB).

How do you know what will happen tomorrow? What, after all, is your life? It is like a puff of smoke visible for a little while and then dissolving into thin air (Jas. 4:14, Phillips).

And I saw a great white throne and the one who sat upon it, from whose face the earth and sky fled away, but they found no place to hide. I saw the dead, great and small, standing before God; and The Books were opened, including the Book of Life. And the dead were judged according to the things written in The Books, each according to the deeds he had done (Rev. 20:11-12, TLB).

From Genesis to Revelation the death knell sounds. The Bible is replete with reminders that we must die. There is one appointment we all must keep—our appointment with death. We haven't kept it yet, but we will.

An old legend tells of a merchant in Bagdad who one day sent his servant to the market. Before very long the servant came back, white and trembling, and in great agitation said to his master: "Down in the market place I was jostled by a woman in the crowd, and when I turned around I saw it was Death that jostled me. She looked at me and made a threatening gesture. Master, please lend me your horse, for I must hasten away to avoid her. I will ride to Samarra and there I will hide, and Death will not find me."

The merchant lent him his horse and the servant galloped away in great haste. Later the merchant went down to the market place and saw Death standing in the crowd. He went over to her and asked, "Why did you frighten my servant this morning? Why did you make a threatening gesture?"

"That was not a threatening gesture," Death said. "It was only a start of surprise. I was astonished to see him in Bagdad, for I have an appointment with him tonight in Samarra."[3]

Yes, all of us have our own appointment in Samarra. Though we may try, the appointment will not be canceled.

But what happens at death? What happens when we keep that appointment? What exactly occurs when life departs from the body? We'll look at that next.

Root Issues

1. Contemplate once again the searching words of Moses' prayer in Psalm 90. Pause at verse 10. If you knew for sure that you would pass from this earth at the age of seventy, how many years of life would you have left? Sobering? Time is a very limited resource, isn't it? Pull out your calculator and take it a step further. How many *days* would that leave you in your life's hourglass . . . how many *hours?* Keying off Moses' words in verse 12, what does it mean to *you*—to your priorities—to present to God "a heart of wisdom"?

2. What incident within the last year reminded you of Paul's assertion in 2 Corinthians 4:16 that "our outward man is decaying," or temporary? Are you living in the reality of the *second* half of that verse? What does the specific phrase "day by day" suggest to you?

3. If you'd like to pass along some of these thoughts about heaven, hell, and our eternal destiny in a concise, "transferable" form, you might want to consider buying several copies of my booklet *DESTINY: Choosing to Change the Course of Your Life* at a Christian bookstore. Give them to those who are considering the issues of knowing Christ. Explain why you want them to read it. After several days get back in touch with them.

4. As you work through the information in this chapter and the others in this section, write down your personal response to what you have encountered. What are your feelings? What did you learn—or relearn? How do you think the Lord might lead you to respond to what you've read?

5. Besides the sobering glimpse into the afterlife provided by Luke 16:19-31, there are some serious matters to consider about *this* life. Do you, for instance, have any "Lazaruses" living near your "front gate"? Near your community? Have you seen the faces of the poor looking at you from the "gate" of your television or magazines in your home? What is the

Growing Deep in the Christian Life: Eternity

danger of habitually closing your eyes and ears to the desperate needs of the poor? Consider some of the following Scriptures and ask the Lord how He might lead you to respond: Matthew 25:31-46; Psalm 82:3-4; Proverbs 14:31; 21:13.

6. Luke 16:29-31 offers startling evidence of the Scripture's power to impact lives. Take a close look at these verses and compare them to the ringing words found in Hebrews 4:12. In what ways could you incorporate this powerful force for God into your daily contacts, correspondence, and conversations?

Extending Your Roots

1. Using a dictionary as a resource, write your definition of *twilight*. Why are topics like grief, immortality, suicide, euthanasia, and out-of-body experiences appropriate for a "twilight zone" study?

2. Read Ecclesiastes 3:1-21. Reflect on each "a time to" phrase.

3. Death will surely come, but when? Read Psalm 90:9-12. What does "live each day as if it were your last" mean to you?

4. Read Paul's description of death in 1 Corinthians 15. Did death appear to be a friend or enemy?

5. What made the difference?

6. List three interesting facts or phrases describing the deaths of:
Aaron, Numbers 20:23-29

Abraham, Genesis 25:1-11

Elijah, 2 Kings 2:1-11

7. The writers of God's Word viewed death in different ways. Describe death as recorded in:
Jeremiah 21:8

Acts 2:24

Hebrews 2:14

Psalm 94:17

Ruth 1:17

 *Taproot*

1. Plan your Christian memorial/funeral service. Do you want a sad or celebrative service?

2. Select the hymns.

3. Do you want your testimony of faith in the Lord Jesus Christ read?

4. Give the completed service to a responsible person for keeping until needed.

2 Resurrection: Promises and Procedure

I'd like for us to turn to the *real* twilight zone and see our future—2 Corinthians, chapter 5.

For Christians

First, let me address you who are Christians. I want to write to you who know that you have eternal life with Jesus Christ. It will help you to think in terms of categories. I want you to think about that which is seen (your body, your outer person) and that which is unseen (your inner person, your soul, your spirit). Think in those categories as we read this analogy of a house which has been torn down. It's a picture of the earthly body when it dies.

> For we know that if the earthly tent which is our house is torn down, we have a building from God, a house not made with hands, eternal in the heavens. For indeed in this house we groan, longing to be clothed with our dwelling from heaven; inasmuch as we, having put it on, shall not be found naked. For indeed while we are in this tent, we groan, being burdened, because we do not want to be unclothed, but to be clothed, in order that what is mortal may be swallowed up by life. Now He who prepared us for this very purpose is God, who gave to us the Spirit as a pledge. Therefore, being always of good courage, and knowing that while we are at home in the body we are absent from the Lord—for we walk by faith, not by sight—we are of good courage, I say, and prefer rather to be absent from the body and to be at home with the Lord (2 Cor. 5:1-8).

Return for a moment to verse 1. God promises us that

there will be some kind of bodily existence, some kind of "eternal house not made with hands" that will be with us throughout eternity. And the point of this passage is that as long as we are living in this earthly body, He postpones giving us our glorified body, called in this passage our "building from God . . . eternal in the heavens." In the waiting period—during our earthly holding pattern—we "groan" (v. 2).

Prior to speaking on this subject recently, I talked with a friend who told me of his daughter who, though not old in years, is now struggling with a tragic disease. I spoke earlier with another friend whose sister has been in a cross-cultural mission ministry for forty-five years. She recently returned to the United States. During an extensive physical examination, the physician found cancer in her abdomen. Two up-to-date illustrations that our bodies "groan." The illustrations could be multiplied by the hundreds every day. You or I may be next!

You discover through the frown of your physician that the x-ray doesn't look good. You are told that the prognosis is bleak. And you're surprised because you're still so young. You didn't expect to be carrying in your body the marks of disease and death. But you do, and you are. The body longs to be changed. And as long as we are present in this groaning body, we are absent from our Lord. That's a major point of these verses: "at home in the body . . . absent from the Lord" (v. 6).

In one word, death means *separation*. When death occurs, the inner part of us is separated from the outer, the soul and spirit depart from the body. That is the simplest description of death—the soul and spirit are instantaneously removed from the physical body. Our "outer shell"—that part of us that pumps blood and breathes, our anatomy comprised of muscle and bone, tendons and organs—that part of us dies and immediately begins to decay. But the inner part of us, the personality, the soul-spirit, the people we really are, the real, albeit invisible, part of us is taken to the presence of the Lord. Did you notice how Paul put it in verse 8?

We are of good courage, I say, and prefer rather to be absent from the body and to be at home with the Lord.

Now this is good news. We who know the Lord Jesus carry about within ourselves a soul and a spirit. It was that part of us which He invaded at the moment we were born from above—when we became Christians. He has taken up residence there, having given us a new nature. He has become a part of our inner being. And even though our outer shell hurts and groans and is dying, our inner person is maturing, awaiting its home with the Lord. That connection occurs the moment we die.

We read elsewhere in the New Testament:

> Therefore we do not lose heart, but though our outer man is decaying, yet our inner man is being renewed day by day. For momentary, light affliction is producing for us an eternal weight of glory far beyond all comparison, while we look not at the things which are seen, but at the things which are not seen; for the things which are seen are temporal, but the things which are not seen are eternal (2 Cor. 4:16-18).

Keep in mind that death always means separation—an instant separation of the soul and spirit from the body. The body (whether cremated or embalmed and placed in a casket or a crypt, or whether it is destroyed in some tragic death) remains on earth as the soul and spirit depart to be with the Lord. So then, what happens to the body?

Job, that venerable, old saint, once wrote:

> For I know that my redeemer liveth, and that he shall stand at the latter day upon the earth: and though after my skin worms destroy this body, yet in my flesh shall I see God (Job 19:25-26, KJV).

He then said, "My eyes will see Him." In other words, at some time in the future, we will be in face-to-face touch with each other.

What did Job have in mind? He envisioned the next phase of the real "Twilight Zone"—the resurrection of the earthly body.

Two verses need to be read together at this point, 2 Corinthians 4:14 and 1 Thessalonians 4:16-17. The former states the promise; the latter, the procedure.

Knowing that He who raised the Lord Jesus will raise us also with Jesus and will present us with you.

For the Lord Himself will descend from heaven with a shout, with the voice of the archangel, and with the trumpet of God; and the dead in Christ shall rise first. Then we who are alive and remain shall be caught up together with them in the clouds to meet the Lord in the air, and thus we shall always be with the Lord.

What helpful insight these two passages provide! Here's the way the after-life procedure will occur. When death takes place, the soul and spirit depart immediately into the presence of the Lord. There is no soul sleep. Neither is there reincarnation nor reentry of any kind. Remember Hebrews 9:27? "It is appointed for men to die once"—to die ONCE. The soul and spirit, having gone instantly into the presence of the Lord, will await the resurrection of the body. When the body is resurrected, the soul and spirit will be joined to that glorified body (which will no longer "groan," or age, or suffer any of its former earthly limitations). It will be fitted for eternity. And in this glorified state, we will spend eternity with our God.

What an encouragement to hang onto! We will have no more tears, no more death, no more sadness, no more crying, no more disease, no more temptations, no more deformity, retardation, or struggle with Satan, no more oppression of any kind. No more paralysis or crippling diseases. None of that! All those things are passed away as eternity dawns. I can hardly imagine how this information must thrill those who have physical or mental handicaps. In a context of perfect peace, physically and personally, all Christians will enjoy the presence of our Lord forever and ever and ever.

That is why the psalmist could declare with such assurance:

Precious in the sight of the Lord Is the death of His godly ones (Ps. 116:15).

Every believer in Jesus Christ who goes home to be with the Lord has this unshakable and marvelous future in front of him or her. Every death is a reminder that the fight against pain has ended. Every burial is a reminder that life is merely a temporary abode for this body. Never, ever doubt it: This body will be raised and will be changed. The more I think about it, the more outstanding this doctrine becomes. What a future God has planned for those who love Him and live lives pleasing to Him! The old gospel song says it well, "O that will be glory for me!"

For Non-Christians

But there is also bad news. The bad news does not relate to those who know the Lord, only to those who do not. Non-Christians face a future that makes this present earthly existence, by comparison, seem like a rose garden.

To grasp the impact of the contrast, we must force ourselves to think in another category. We've considered the future of the believer who dies. The body is placed in the grave awaiting the resurrection when it will be joined with the soul-spirit. And that wonderful union will be in a glorified, peaceful state forever with the Lord. But what about the nonbeliever? Let's allow Scripture to speak, rather than human opinion.

The New Testament is not silent about the destiny of the unbeliever. You may be surprised to know that the Bible says much more about hell than it does about heaven. It is possible to develop a rather clear and concise theology of hell; though when we come to the subject of heaven, much of it is left to one's imaginative, interpretive, creative thoughts. But there's no guesswork when it comes to the destiny of the damned.

But when the Son of Man comes in His glory, and all the angels with Him, then He will sit on His glorious throne. And all the nations will be gathered before Him; and He will separate them from one another, as the shepherd separates the sheep from the goats. Then He will also say to those on His left, "Depart from Me, accursed ones, into the eternal fire which has been prepared for the devil and his angels" (Matt. 25:31-32,41).

That is an interesting statement. Tragic, yes, but interesting. The place that was originally prepared for the devil and his demonic host will one day also include those "accursed ones" who lived their lives apart from faith in Christ Jesus.

You will observe the reference in Matthew 25:41 to "eternal fire." It means just what it says. Even the universalist John Robinson, who wrote the book *But This I Can't Believe,* had to admit that it is futile to attempt to prove Christ taught no belief in hell or eternal punishment.

Extending Your Roots

1. Read Job 19:25-26. What would your face-to-face encounter with God be like if it came today? Find a hymn about the Redeemer and meditate on the words or sing the hymn.

2. Through His death and resurrection, Jesus prepared a way of victory for us. List the victory in the following verses: Romans 6:6-10

Revelation 1:17-18

2 Timothy 1:10

Hebrews 2:14-15

3. The destiny of the unbeliever/non-Christian is clearly defined in God's Word. Read the passages about death and

resurrection experiences from the Scripture and record the destiny:
John 5:25-29

John 8:24

Hosea 13:13

Revelation 20:11-15

4. Why is it so difficult for some people to believe what Jesus said in John 11:26?

5. Explain in positive and negative terms what resurrection and life mean for those who trust in Christ and those who do not trust in Christ.

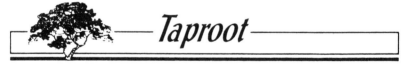
Taproot

1. Using a Bible dictionary and a Bible encyclopedia as references, study the doctrine of resurrection. List specific teachings that are new to your understanding.

3 Destiny: Hell or Heaven

When the unbelieving person dies, the body (as with the believer) begins to decay. It is either cremated or placed in a grave, or perhaps in death it was blown apart—whatever. However, the soul and spirit of the unsaved, rather than going into paradise—the place of God's presence—go to Gehenna, called Hades in the New Testament or, more often, "hell." It is a place of temporary, conscious pain. I say temporary because it, too, awaits final resurrection of the body.

Now before I go any further, let me say that many who hear such a thing become fearful and respond quickly by thinking, "I need to get more religious. I need to go to church more. I need to start carrying a Bible. I need to start doing a lot of good works. I have to deal with this guilt that I'm living with. So maybe if I get religion, I'll escape this eternity that frightens me."

Remember the scribes and Pharisees? They were the most religious people who ever lived. For all who think religion is going to help, read again what Jesus said to these religious people who were living in hypocrisy, mouthing mere words about their faith:

> You serpents, you brood of vipers, how shall you escape the sentence of hell? (Matt. 23:33).

Religion doesn't relieve anyone from the future of hell. Neither does going to church, studying the Bible, being baptized, paying your bills, living a good life, obeying the law, or contributing great sums of money to the church or some other good cause. None of that will ingratiate anyone before a holy God who requires perfect righteousness, not human goodness. You read that correctly; He requires *perfect* righteousness. And not even religious people can provide that kind of righteousness. Righteousness that equips us for eternal life comes only through the Lord Jesus Christ.

Christ spoke of another response in Mark, chapter 9. Many people will excuse themselves by saying, "I'm only human. I can't help it if I've got these eyes that lust . . . I've got these hands that commit wrong . . . I have these feet that take me to ungodly places. I walk in darkness, not in light, but I'm a helpless victim of my own humanity." What did Jesus say about all that?

> And if your hand causes you to stumble, cut it off; it is better for you to enter life crippled, than having your two hands, to go into hell, into the unquenchable fire.
> And if your foot causes you to stumble, cut it off; it is better for you to enter life lame, than having your two feet, to be cast into hell.
> And if your eye causes you to stumble, cast it out; it is better for you to enter the kingdom of God with one eye, than having two eyes, to be cast into hell (Mark 9:43,45,47).

There are times you take the Bible literally; there are also times you understand that it is using symbolism or accommodating terminology, as here. Jesus isn't saying that we're to enter life with no hands, no feet, and no eyes. His terms are severe and superextreme to communicate His point. He is saying it is foolish for us to hide behind the lame excuse of a hand or an eye or a foot that disobeys. You prepare yourself by preparing your heart. You prepare yourself by placing your whole self at the disposal of Jesus Christ who cleanses hands, eyes, heart, feet, the whole life. But it's worth noting that He refers not once, not twice, but three times in a row to hell, which is a place "Where the worm does not die, and the fire is not quenched" (v. 48).

Look further at John, chapter 5. Jesus is speaking again.

> Truly, truly, I say unto you, an hour is coming and now is, when the dead shall hear the voice of the Son of God; and

those who hear shall live. For just as the Father has life in Himself, even so He gave to the Son also to have life in Himself; and He gave Him authority to execute judgment, because He is the Son of Man. Do not marvel at this; for an hour is coming, in which all who are in the tombs shall hear His voice, and shall come forth; those who did the good deeds to a resurrection of life, those who committed the evil deeds to a resurrection of judgment (John 5:25-29).

There is no getting around it. Unless you wish to do an enormous amount of semantic footwork, or you have an airtight scheme of cutting out certain Scriptures that make you feel uncomfortable, you're left with some pretty damaging evidence. And I would suggest that we not joke any longer about hell. Many other things may be, but hell is not a laughing matter—though many laugh to nullify hell's significance.

The following quotation may seem a little blunt, but the author has an excellent point. Don't let his abrupt approach dull the edge of that point.

It is not unlikely that within the last twenty-four hours you've heard someone say, "What the hell are you doing?" Or, "I sure as hell will." Or, "Who in the hell do you think you are?"

That word *hell* has become a conversational byword in our day. Good friends dare to say playfully to one another, "Go to hell." They surely don't mean, "Go to the place of punishment for the wicked after death," though that is how the dictionary defines the word *hell.*

But why use the word *hell?* Why not instead, "What the jail are you doing?" Or, "I sure as school will." And why not say, "Oh, go to Chicago"? Simply because *jail, school,* and *Chicago,* even for the enemies of each, have no real sting. They have only the flavor of vanilla at a time when chocolate or peppermint is needed.

When it comes right down to it, in the English language, *hell* is the strongest expletive available that carries the idea of ultimate deprivation, devastation, fear, torment, punishment, suffering, and loss. Whether or not the user of the term *hell* believes in an actual, literal hell is of little or no consequence. There is an inbuilt, inarticulated, yet understood bite in the very word itself.

So if hell really is the place for eternal punishment of the wicked after death, how come it's used so lightly millions and millions of times each day? Why is there such an apparent lack of seriousness about the word? Why is a word so heavy with meaning used so indifferently? Why do people pretend the place doesn't exist?

When is the last time you heard a serious sermon on the subject or read an article of note dealing with judgment and eternal punishment? Even the evangelical crowd has, by and large, avoided the topic—opting for a more "positive" approach. Hell has come on hard times.

Deep below the surface of things, a proliferating erosion concerning the seriousness of hell, brought on by a complex web of modern ideas about hell, has stripped this weighty word of most of its awesomely solemn content.[1]

Truth is not always comforting and easy to hear. But I would not be a true servant of God or a loyal ambassador of His will if I failed to tell you the truth about hell. Furthermore, you would be ill-informed regarding your future if all you chose to read in the Bible were only those passages regarding heaven. It is true that there is a certain destiny for the saved. It is called "Paradise," "at home with the Lord," "God's presence," or "heaven." It is also true that there is a certain destiny for the lost. It is called "Hades," "hell," or "the lake of fire."

I suggest we stop using any of those terms lightly. We should reserve the word *hell* for its singular purpose—the destiny of the lost. It is the most hideous scene the mind can imagine, though it isn't imaginary. It is the worst possible place ever prepared for anyone's existence.

The ultimate scene is in the final five verses of Revelation, chapter 20. You owe it to yourself to take a look. You may not like what you see, but when you read Revelation 20:11-15, you'll be reading the truth. Let's understand where we are before we attempt to imagine this awful scene. Perhaps a little review will help.

When the *believer* dies, the body does into the grave; the soul and spirit go immediately to be with the Lord Jesus awaiting the body's resurrection, when they're joined together to be forever with the Lord in eternal bliss. When the *unbeliever* dies, the body goes to the grave, while the soul and the spirit of that body go into Hades or hell where it is kept in conscious torment (which we shall study in chapter 7). Those souls in hell are awaiting the resurrection of the body, which will occur immediately before the last judgment. That particular judgment is the judgment for the lost—the scene portrayed in Revelation 20.

> And I saw a great white throne and Him who sat upon it, from whose presence earth and heaven fled away, and no place was found for them (v. 11).

We're looking at a scene that will occur somewhere in space. There is no longer any earth. It's been burned up. There is no longer the atmospheric heavens as we know of them. This incredible scene is not some imaginary twilight zone, but the ultimate *real* twilight zone.

> And I saw the dead, the great and the small, standing before the throne, and books were opened; and another book was opened, which is the book of life; and the dead were judged from the things which were written in the books, according to their deeds. And the sea gave up the dead which were in it, and death and Hades gave up the dead which were in them; and they were judged, every one of them according to their deeds. And death and Hades were thrown into the lake of fire. This is the second death, the lake of fire (vv. 12-14).

Technically, the ultimate abode of the lost is not hell. Hell itself is only a temporary location of the damned. The eternal abode of the lost is the lake of fire, the destiny of all who die without faith in the Lord Jesus Christ.

> And if anyone's name was not found written in the book of life, he was thrown into the lake of fire (v. 15).

Extending Your Roots

1. David and Solomon were concerned about their destiny. Read and paraphrase Psalm 39:4 and Ecclesiastes 9:10.

2. The Pharisees and scribes expected to escape hell (Matt. 23:33) because of their religion. From the Gospels, list the religious characteristics of these people. Why is righteousness more important than religion?

Now check your answer using these verses:

1 John 3:10
Matthew 5:6
2 Timothy 4:8
Romans 5:18

3. For a clearer picture of the destiny of the lost, read the following references:
Psalm 88

Matthew 16:18

Jeremiah 7:31-32

Job 10:21-22

Luke 16:19-31

Matthew 5:22

2 Peter 2:4

Destiny: Heaven or Hell

Revelation 20:11-15

4. If you needed to tell a lost person the truth about hell, what would you say?

 *Taproot*

What lies beyond history? At least four things will occur. Write a brief descriptive paragraph about each.

1. There will be judgment (Matt. 25).

2. There will be the resurrected life (Acts 24:15).

3. There will be a heaven and a hell.

4. There will be a new order (Rev. 21:1; 2 Peter 3:10,13).

4 | Preparation: Response and Result

With no desire to play on your emotions or manipulate some response from you, I must communicate the truth for all who read this book. There are two very important facts that everyone must face. The *first:* The only time to prepare for then is NOW. The *second:* There is no chance of change after death. I've not been writing of some playful, imaginary, and entertaining scene. I've been dealing with truth and reality painful to read and, I can assure you, unpleasant to write. I do not care what you were told as you were being raised, or what you have been taught later on by whomever. According to an intelligent and careful study of the Scripture, I can assure you on the authority of the Word of God, this is the truth. You must prepare for it now since there is no chance of changing things after you die.

What is the issue? I turn, finally, to the letter of 1 John to answer that question. John explains the issue in simple terms. It is relatively simple to read and easy to grasp, but the question is: Will you believe it?

> The one who believes in the Son of God has the witness in himself; the one who does not believe God has made Him a liar, because he has not believed in the witness that God has borne concerning His Son. And the witness is this, that God has given us eternal life, and this life is in His Son. He who has the Son has the life; he who does not have the Son of God does not have the life. These things I have written to you who believe in the name of the Son of God, in order that you may know that you have eternal life (1 John 5:10-13).

Don't misunderstand. *Everybody* has eternal life because everyone has an eternal soul. The issue is not, "Do I have eternal life?" It is, rather, "Where will I spend my eternal life?" If the most exciting moment of your life is *behind* you, you're lost. If the most exciting moment of your life is still *in front* of you, you're saved.

Three men were the closest of friends. They enjoyed the outdoors and often hunted and fished together. On this occasion they found themselves around a fire in Northern India, drinking coffee and watching the distant light of early dawn. Several weeks before this trip, the oldest of the three men had become a Christian. He had not yet had the opportunity to share the excitement of his new destiny with the others.

As they sat around the fire they began talking about their various adventures. One of the younger men suggested they each answer the same question—What's the most exciting experience in all your life?—by sharing some intriguing story.

The first man to answer told of the tiger hunt he'd been on . . . about how they had to stalk the beast for more than two days. The final six hours were the most thrilling when he found himself face to face with that big cat. Just as the hungry animal leaped, he fired. The cat lay dead . . . but he thought he was going to die of fright.

The second hunter told of an experience in Alaska, north of the Aleutian Islands, involving an enormous bear. He said it all happened so fast that it wasn't until the whole experience was over that he realized how close to death he had been. He had to squeeze off three final rounds before that huge beast finally dropped virtually at his feet. He reminded them that the furry, skinned bear was now a rug covering the floor in his den.

Finally, the oldest man spoke. "My most exciting experience? It hasn't happened yet. But it will occur only seconds after I die." This led into an opportunity to talk with his closest friends about Christ. They listened with rapt attention as he described the thrilling anticipation he never knew before. Death was no longer a fearful thing on the distant horizon—but rather an entrance into the most awesome delight the mind can imagine.

The crisp voice of Rod Serling is no longer heard. He's dead. And every time I hear the haunting melody of *The Twilight Zone,* I wonder where Rod Serling is today. I really wonder.

Extending Your Roots

1. The disciples stood on the Mount of Olives and watched Jesus ascend into heaven. Recall what Jesus had promised them in John 14.

2. On six separate occasions (recorded in Acts 22—26) between Paul's third missionary journey and his trip to Rome, he stood before different audiences and presented Christ to them. Outline the method Paul used each time.

3. In a sense, death is like the twilight zone (what happens is not clearly defined.) However, God's Word clearly defines what death cannot do.

Read the following verses and make a list of things that death cannot do.

Romans 8:35-39

1 Thessalonians 4:13-18

Preparation: Response and Result

1 Corinthians 15:21-57

John 11:25-26

Taproot

1. Read again the story in this section of the book about the three men on a hunting trip. What you would do or say if you had his opportunity?

5 | An Interview with One from Beyond

As late as the 1960s, Americans were known as a death-denying culture. Our opinions were traditional. Our views were antiquated. Worst of all, our lips were sealed.

When loved ones were told that their disease was terminal, only the closest stayed near until the end. It was virtually unheard of to bring the dying home. They remained isolated in hospitals and "rest homes." And when death came, isolation turned to awkward silence. Few words were said as we buried the dead while the world rushed on.

This inability to face such grim realities was not overlooked by everyone, however. A ground swell of concern refused to remain still much longer.

By April of 1970, a few brave souls broke the silence barrier. In a rare and long overdue article on death in America, a national news magazine lamented the fact that we are guilty of denying this reality. Their words penetrated. They became like the ever-enlarging hole in the dike as more and more information began to flow from the media. It was only eight years later that the same publication titled its cover "Living with Dying," heralding a newfound interest in the study of death—a subject no longer shrouded in mute mystery.

What Broke the Barrier?

Anyone my age or older would want to know what broke the barrier. What caused us to come out of the closet? What helped us to stop denying? Surely it was more than a magazine article. At least four causes have contributed to the change.

1. The Medical Profession. Within the past two decades the medical profession has focused increased interest on death and dying. Books, research, seminars, and journal reports (especially out-of-body experiences—OBE—and euthanasia) have begun to flow from competent physicians. These professionals have become more candid regarding their struggles with the issues as well as more willing to dialogue with other professionals and research scientists.

2. The Educational World. As I mentioned earlier, educational curricula have begun to include courses on death and dying. Medical schools, distinguished universities, community colleges, and high schools alike are addressing the subject. Some go so far as to take field trips to mortuaries, or interview those who have had OBE.

3. The Media. No one can overlook the ever-growing number of films, plays, radio talk shows, and new stories that now emphasize death-related issues. Within the last two years there have been numerous television programs focusing attention on subjects once considered unmentionable.

4. Public Interest. Patients who were once given up as dead are now kept alive through new techniques and equipment. Questions are now being asked by the public that weren't even thought of three decades ago:

- Who should be allowed to "pull the plug"?
- Why can't my loved one die at home?
- What are the telltale signals of potential suicide?
- When is it acceptable to end one's own life of pain?
- How can we say that "afterlife visions" aren't reliable?

First, perhaps it would help to make a few observations about deathbed phenomena and afterlife visions.

Several Common Death-and-Dying Events

A physician, Dr. Marshall Goldberg, has interviewed many patients resuscitated from cardiac arrest. Since it takes three or four minutes for the brain to die after the heart ceases to function, some patients (interviewed before a rapidly developing amnesia effaces the memory) have related some remarkable visions, feelings, sounds, and related OBE. A few of the more recurrent descriptions include:

• Surprisingly peaceful surroundings

• An almost sound-proof, pain-deadening "curtain" that descends

• "Flashbacks," in which one's entire life passes in review—one person referred to it as "an autobiographical slide show"

• Bright light, warm feelings, buzzing and ringing sounds[1]

If this subject fascinates you, there are a couple of books I could recommend which are reliable works: *Life After Life* by Raymond Moody, Jr., M.D., and *Life, Death, and Beyond* by J. Kerby Anderson. I'd like to quote from both of these sources before we turn to the Scriptures for even deeper insight:

Dr. Moody writes:

> Despite the wide variation in the circumstances surrounding close calls with death and in the types of persons undergoing them, it remains true that there is a striking similarity among the accounts of the experiences themselves. In fact, the similarities among various reports are so great that one can easily pick out about fifteen separate elements which recur again and again in the mass of narratives that I have collected. On the basis of these points of likeness, let me now reconstruct a brief, theoretically "ideal" or "complete" experience which embodies all of the common elements, in the order in which it is typical for them to occur.
>
> A man is dying and, as he reaches the point of greatest physical distress, he hears himself pronounced dead by his doctor. He begins to hear an uncomfortable noise, a loud ringing or buzzing, and at the same time feels himself moving very rapidly through a long, dark tunnel. After this, he suddenly finds himself outside his own physical body, but still in the immediate physical environment, and he sees his own body from a distance, as though he is a spectator. He

watches the resuscitation attempt from this unusual vantage point and is in a state of emotional upheaval.

After a while, he collects himself and becomes more accustomed to his odd condition. He notices he still has a "body," but one of a very different nature and with very different powers from the physical body he has left behind. Soon other things begin to happen. Others come to meet and to help him. He glimpses the spirits of relatives and friends who have already died, and a loving, warm spirit of a kind he has never encountered before—a being of light—appears before him. This being asks him a question, nonverbally, to make him evaluate his life and helps him along by showing him a panoramic, instantaneous playback of the major events of his life. At some point he finds himself approaching some sort of barrier or border, apparently representing the limit between earthly life and the next life. Yet he finds that he must go back to the earth, that the time for his death had not yet come. At this point he resists, for by now he is taken up with his experiences in the afterlife and does not want to return. He is overwhelmed by intense feelings of joy, love, and peace. Despite his attitude, though, he somehow reunites with his physical body and lives.

Later he tries to tell others, but he has trouble doing so. In the first place, he can find no human words adequate to describe these unearthly episodes. He also finds that others scoff, so he stops telling other people. Still, the experience affects his life profoundly, especially his views about death and its relationship to life.[2]

And one more comment from J. Kerby Anderson:

Those who have been involved in research on out-of-body experiences [OBE] have noted a very interesting phenomenon. Even when a person is having an OBE, he is still in contact with his body. He is attached to his body by means of a "cord." On one of his out-of-body excursions, Robert Monroe describes looking for the cord that connected his physical body with his Second Body.

I turned to look for the "cord" but it was not visible to me; either it was too dark or not there. Then I reached around my head to see if I could feel it coming out the front, top, or back of my head. As I reached the back of my head, my hands brushed against something and I felt behind me with both hands. Whatever it was extended out from a spot in my back directly between my shoulder blades. . . . I reached outward, and it formed into a "cord," if you can call a two-inch-thick cable a "cord."

Such a phenomenon is not limited to out-of-body experiences. It has also been reported by those at a deathbed.[3]

Because of the increasing number of similar reports, it is to the point where one wonders if there might be something to all these OBE accounts. I am not ready to say that all of these things actually occur, but, quite frankly, I am unable to ignore how much in agreement they are. It's the similarity of them that I find so intriguing.

Extending Your Roots

1. Read Psalm 90:9-12. Why would the psalmist pray, "teach us to number our days"? List some concrete ways to "number our days."

2. Place a check mark beside the three most common reminders of death and explain your thoughts.

driving by a cemetery
hearing an ambulance siren
certain hymns
the death of a peer
seeing a funeral procession
reading a familiar name in the obituary column
visiting an older person

3. The apostle Paul found himself caught between wanting to live and wanting to die. Read Philippians 1:19-24. Using a commentary, study this Christian paradox. What does "living with dying" mean to you? Explain.

 *Taproot*

The barriers to understanding death and talking about death are broken down by awareness.

Select two of the suggested projects and seek to complete the assignment within one month from today.

1. Locate and read a recent medical article on death and dying. Apply a Bible verse or Bible story to your article. (This may be difficult, but give it a try.)

2. Watch for lectures on death and dying. Plan to attend. Or visit a local mortuary. Become aware of the process of preparing a body for burial.

3. Watch for death-related issues on television, particularly out-of-body experiences. View video movies about death. (Numerous movies are available.) Observe the behavior of the people involved in the story.

4. Select a controversial subject such as removing life support, commiting suicide, dying at home, or helping a person die. Become aware of barriers to these practices.

5. The age-old question is: Where does death come from? Read Genesis 2:15-17 and 3:17-19. Using a chain-reference Bible locate other cross-references to this passage. Respond to this question: Why should I have to die just because Adam and Eve sinned?

6. Read again the section "Several Common Death-and-Dying Events." The Bible records events where someone was involved in telling a person or group of people they were dying. Read Jeremiah 9:17-24 and find the following information:
Scenario:
Dilemma:
Solution:

Growing Deep in the Christian Life: Eternity

7. Now pretend you have the responsibility of telling a person he or she is dying. What would you say?

8. Consider this question: Should a dying person be told? Explain your answer.

6 | Biblical Hope for Christians to Claim

I am grateful that we aren't limited to opinions of observers and feelings of people on deathbeds. The Scripture addresses the subject often and freely. These scriptural passages provide us with great peace when the chilling winds of death blow near us. Each one gives the Christian hope and comfort. Here are several pertinent passages:

> Now He who prepared us for this very purpose is God, who gave to us the Spirit as a pledge, Therefore, being always of good courage, and knowing that while we re at home in the body we are absent from the Lord—for we walk by faith, not by sight—we are of good courage, I say, and prefer rather to be absent from the body and to be at home with the Lord (2 Cor. 5:5-8).

> Precious in the sight of the Lord is the death of His godly ones (Ps. 116:15).

> Now I say this, brethren, that flesh and blood cannot inherit the kingdom of God; nor does the perishable inherit the imperishable. Behold, I tell you a mystery; we shall not all sleep, but we shall all be changed, in a moment, in the twinkling of an eye, at the last trumpet; for the trumpet will sound, and the dead will be raised imperishable, and we shall be changed. For this perishable must put on the imperishable, and this mortal must put on immortality. But when this perishable will have put on the imperishable, and this mortal will have put on immortality, then will come about the saying that is written, "Death is swallowed up in victory. O death, where is your victory? O death, where is your sting?" The sting of death is sin, and the power of sin is the

law; but thanks be to God, who gives us the victory through our Lord Jesus Christ. Therefore, my beloved brethren, be steadfast, immovable, always abounding in the work of the Lord, knowing that your toil is not in vain in the Lord (1 Cor. 15:50-58).

But we do not want you to be uninformed, brethren, about those who are asleep, that you may not grieve, as do the rest who have no hope. For if we believe that Jesus died and rose again, even so God will bring with Him those who have fallen asleep in Jesus. For this we say to you by the word of the Lord, that we who are alive, and remain until the coming of the Lord, shall not precede those who have fallen asleep. For the Lord Himself will descend from heaven with a shout, with the voice of the archangel, and with the trumpet of God, and the dead in Christ shall rise first. Then we who are alive and remain shall be caught up together with them in the clouds to meet the Lord in the air, and thus we shall always be with the Lord. Therefore comfort one another with these words (1 Thess. 4:13-18).

And I heard a loud voice from the throne, saying, "Behold, the tabernacle of God is among men, and He shall dwell among them, and they shall be His people, and God Himself shall be among them, and He shall wipe away every tear from their eyes; and there shall no longer be any death; there shall no longer be any mourning, or crying, or pain; the first things have passed away" (Rev. 21:3-4).

And there shall no longer be any night; and they shall not have need of the light of a lamp nor the light of the sun, because the Lord God shall illumine them; and they shall reign forever and ever (Rev. 22:5).

Remember this: Every time you attend a funeral or memorial service, you are merely viewing the physical remains of the deceased individual. You are seeing only the body, which is decaying, decomposing. You are not viewing the person—only the outer "shell." Regardless of how we refer to the remains—slumbering, at rest, at peace—or how "natural" he or she may look, we are looking at that which is going to be changed and glorified, renewed so that the body can endure eternity. As we learned in the previous chapter, the soul-spirit, that invisible part of the Christian, has been taken to be in the presence of the Lord. What you are seeing before you is the external "suit of clothes"; or as 2 Corinthians 5 calls it, you're seeing "the house" which is now destroyed. The funeral service provides us a time to give God thanks for the memory of the person and for the fact that the body will be raised some day in the future.

One of my favorite lines that I often state once the funeral party gathers at the grave site is related to that future day when the dead will be raised. I will usually say, "Whether you realize it or not, at this very moment you are standing on resurrection ground." (I've actually seen people look down, then step aside two or three feet!)

There will be a time when the graves will be opened and the bodies will be removed in a glorified state to be forever with the Lord Jesus. Plain and simple, the Christian has no reason to fear death since the future is so full of hope and happiness. Even though we cannot turn to any Scripture that states that a believer was interviewed after death, we know these things are true.

Extending Your Roots

1. Let's think about some customs related to funerals and memorial services. Several customs are presented in the Bible. Read the biblical reference and write what custom was practiced.
Genesis 50:1-13

Jeremiah 9:17-18; 34:5

Amos 5:16

1 Samuel 31:12-13

Luke 7:12

John 11:14

Mark 16:1

Matthew 27:59

Acts 9:34

2. Are any of these customs observed today?
3. Describe a funeral or memorial service you have attended recently. Think of one tradition that you observed.

 *Taproot*

1. Jesus is the center of hope for the Christian. Read 1 Corinthians 15:12-33 and Job 14:1-14. Make a list of the key thoughts about hope from these verses.

2. Select a hymn about hope and sing or meditate on the words.

7 Ultimate Realities for Non-Christians to Face

There is an extremely vivid account in the Bible where an *unbeliever* is interviewed. Don't misunderstand, we're not going to read of another fascinating OBE, but a startling narrative of the afterlife related by the ultimate authority on the subject—the Son of God Himself.

A number of commentators refer to Luke 16:19-31 as a parable. I'm not so sure. By naming two of the key characters in the account, I believe that Jesus gives us ample reason to interpret these verses as an actual historical event. A true story of two men . . . and their eternal destinies.

Luke sets the stage:

> Now there was a certain rich man, and he habitually dressed in purple and fine linen, gaily living in splendor every day. And a certain poor man named Lazarus was laid at his gate, covered with sores, and longing to be fed with the crumbs which were falling from the rich man's table; besides, even the dogs were coming and licking his sores (vv. 19-21).

It is a pathetic scene. First there is a rich man who, as we shall see, is eternally lost. Then there is a poor man who is eternally saved. They live in two different worlds in their earthly lives. But there is a remarkable change of events at death. Death, the greatest of all levelers, reduces everything to the lowest common denominator. Look at the way Jesus describes the reversal of roles:

> Now it came about that the poor man died and he was carried away by the angels to Abraham's bosom; and the rich man also died and was buried (v. 22).

When Lazarus, the believer, died, his body was probably tossed in the local dump, the refuse pile. Chances are good he didn't even receive a decent burial. But his soul and spirit were taken immediately into the presence of the Lord, called here "Abraham's bosom."

When we read, "The rich man also died and was buried," we can be sure his burial was one of great pomp and elaborate ceremony. So much for his body. It is his eternal soul that interests us. We find him "in Hades" as we continue to read Jesus' words:

> And in Hades he lifted up his eyes, being in torment, and saw Abraham far away, and Lazarus in his bosom (v. 23).

In the verses that follow, we will not read of some paranormal experience reported by a man who saw lights and heard buzzing. This, I believe, is an event, not a vision. It becomes an interview, as it were.

Notice several things that occur. First, there is agony. There is literal pain. He is in torment. And somehow he catches a glimpse of those who are at peace. Second, he is fully conscious. Third, he not only has his senses, he has his memory. Neither is obliterated by death.

> And he cried out and said, "Father Abraham, have mercy on me, and send Lazarus, that he may dip the tip of his finger in water and cool off my tongue, for I am in agony in this flame" (v. 24).

The scene becomes increasingly bleak. Scripture pulls no punches. Earlier it mentioned "torment." Now it's "agony." Observe that the man could reason. He could also visualize his surroundings. He had feeling. He could hear. He could taste. It was as if he still had a tongue.

Abraham (who seems to speak for the Lord) answers the man's request in verse 25:

Child, remember that during your life you received your good things, and likewise Lazarus bad things; but now he is being comforted here, and you are in agony.

Now for those who joke about hell and say, "Well, we'll be there for a while and somebody will just pray us out," take a good look at the next verse:

And besides all this, between us and you there is a great chasm fixed, in order that those who wish to come over from here to you may not be able, and that none may cross over from there to us (v. 26).

The "fixed chasm" suggests a perpetual situation. In other words, it is impossible to change destinies or to escape one's location after death. Even if others wish for you to be released, they cannot come to your rescue. Realizing this, the man begins to bargain.

And he said, "Then I beg you, Father, that you send him to my father's house— " (v. 27).

Now this is where the account becomes extremely moving. The man in torment remembers his family at home. His concern for them is enormous, and understandably so.

"for I have five brothers—that he may warn them, lest they also come to this place of torment" (v. 28).

Let me interrupt the story long enough to ask a question. Is it your feeling that the lost who are dead care about the lost who are alive? If you're uncertain about your answer, read verse 28 again. Since he was unable to escape, his number-one concern was that someone might go to his brothers and communicate the truth about hell to those who are still living. Don't miss the urgency, ". . . that he may warn them." Talk about a missionary message! Talk about evangelistic zeal! If it exists nowhere else, an evangelistic passion exists in hell. "Oh, that someone could go to my brothers . . . if only someone could rise from the dead and appear to my five brothers who are living like I lived, denying what I denied."

This certainly silences the superficial comments we hear

from some who joke, "Aw, I'll just be in hell with all my buddies." All it takes is a few verses from this account to realize there's no companionship there. On the contrary, there is an awful, gnawing, inescapable loneliness.

In response to the man's request, Abraham says to him, "They have Moses and the Prophets." Meaning what? They have the Scripture, the very Word of God. They have God's voice in God's Book. In other words, "Let them who are alive hear the truth of Scripture." Applying it to our day, "They have ample opportunity to hear the truth. Let them pick up the Bible and read it for themselves. Let them hear the preachers. Let them hear the broadcasts. Let them hear the gospel as it is contained in God's Word."

He pleads with greater intensity:

> But he said, "No, Father Abraham, but if someone goes to them from the dead, they will repent!" (v. 30).

"Father Abraham," he reasons, "I know they've got God's Word. But it would make a greater impact if someone were to go to them from the dead. They'd repent. They'd believe. That's all it would take."

I find the following response nothing short of remarkable:

> But he said to him, "If they do not listen to Moses and the Prophets, neither will they be persuaded if someone rises from the dead" (v. 31).

You talk about the power of the Scripture! If you could bring someone back from beyond—someone who has been in hell—to tell people what the future holds, it would not be as effective as Holy Scripture! The most invincible, convincing power on earth is the Word of God as the Holy Spirit uses the truth to convince the lost.

We have sufficient truth available to us in our Bibles to do the job. It is all that is needed to convince people without Christ that they are missing what life is about. Even if we could do something miraculous, like bring someone back from beyond, it would not have as great an impact as simply presenting the Scriptures.

They have Moses and the Prophets ... (v. 29). . . . If they do not listen to Moses and the Prophets, neither will they be persuaded if someone rises from the dead (v. 31).

If I were asked to put the message of this entire chapter into one sentence, it would not contain more than twenty-one words: *Those who ignore the Word of God in life will not be ignored by the God of the Word in eternity.*

Extending Your Roots

1. To examine the ultimate realities of the eternally lost and eternally saved, prepare an intensive Bible study on Luke 16:19-31. Use all available biblical resources. Include in your study a contrast between

   A BELIEVER   and   A NONBELIEVER

2. Locate definitions for *angels, Abraham's bosom, Hades,* and other unfamiliar words.

3. What is meant by "Moses and the Prophets?"

3. Write a brief concluding statement about what you learned from this passage.

Growing Deep in the Christian Life: Eternity

1. Prepare a sermon or devotional using the text from Luke 16:19-31. Develop a theme and three points of an outline.

Theme:

I.

II.

III.

Prayer:

2. Plan an emphasis for your sermon, such as evangelism, loss of loved ones, life-after-death, witnessing, outreach, and others. Select hymns and special music for your sermon or devotional. Conclude with a written prayer related to your theme. Read aloud your finished assignment.

8 | Major Questions Worth Answering

If I were sitting where you're sitting, having read what you have been reading about death and eternity, I believe I would have four or five questions hanging in my head. I have an idea what they might be. So, before we leave this section on resurrection, let's consider several significant concerns.

1. How can a loving God send people to hell? The way that question is worded bothers me. Even though it is commonly asked that way, I don't like the way it sounds, because I don't like what it implies. So if you'll allow me to analyze the question before I answer it, I think it will help.

The question seems to imply that God is indulgent and a bit impotent . . . and that mankind is being taken advantage of, handled cruelly, and treated unfairly—with very little feeling on God's part. Almost like God is taking delight in watching people squirm, saying, "Get out of My sight," as He pushes people into hell against their wills. So if that is what is meant by the question, then that needs to be dealt with first. Suffice it to say, that is *not* what Scripture teaches.

But if it's an honest question, where you wrestle with God's loving character and hell's awful consequences, then I would begin by saying that God has established the ground rules. That's His sovereign right. As the Creator of life, His divine rule states that those who believe in His Son will have eternal life with Him. Those who do not believe in His Son will not have eternal life with Him. The believers will have the blessedness of heaven. Those who reject the message must face the punishment of that rejection.

And lest you think God is calloused and unconcerned over that scene, you'll need to return to 2 Peter 3:9, which states:

> The Lord is not slow about His promise, as some count slowness, but is patient toward you, not wishing for any to perish but for all to come to repentance.

Never forget that verse! When someone presents to you the idea that God cruelly and gleefully dances about heaven as the last people are dumped against their will into hell, remind them of Peter's words. With patience and grace He offers the gift of eternal life and heaven to all who will accept it. Those who refuse the gift He offers must suffer the consequences, having made their own decision about eternity.

2. *What about those who have never heard?* Or, *What about those who sincerely follow their own beliefs and their own religion?* We must always be careful about stepping into the role of God. Only He knows the destiny of people. People you and I may think are in the family may not be . . . and vice versa.

God alone knows the heart. He alone is the One who makes the final determination. Not all who call Him Lord will enter into the kingdom. And conversely, not all who think they are lost are actually lost. Some have genuinely come to know Christ and live under the misguided assumption that they've lost their salvation.

But to answer the question, we need to read again the words of Romans 10 in order to determine the basis of salvation.

> That if you confess with your mouth Jesus as Lord, and believe in your heart that God raised Him from the dead, you shall be saved; for with the heart man believes, resulting in righteousness, and with the mouth he confesses, resulting in salvation. For the Scripture says, "Whoever believes in Him will not be disappointed." For there is no distinction between Jew and Greek; for the same Lord is Lord of all, abounding in

riches for all who call upon Him; for "Whoever will call *upon* the name of the Lord will be saved." How then shall they call upon Him in whom they have not believed? And how shall they believe in Him whom they have not heard? And how shall they hear without a preacher? And how shall they preach unless they are sent? Jesus Just as it is written, "How beautiful are the feet of those who bring glad tidings of good things!"

However, they did not heed the glad tidings; for Isaiah says, "Lord, who has believed our report?" So faith comes from hearing, and hearing by the word of Christ (vv. 9-17).

The only way to have eternal life with God is through faith in the Lord Jesus Christ. God has wonderful ways of getting our attention. He uses natural phenomena. He uses general revelation. He uses circumstance, blessing, and suffering. He uses people. He uses written material. He uses human beings who make the messages known. He will use tragedies and calamities, the loss of a loved one, a crippling disease, bankruptcy, divorce, and a hundred other situations. The marvel of His plan is that He has an endless number of ways of reaching the lost. As they are reached, as the Holy Spirit uses the truth of Scripture to convince them, they will believe.

While I'm on this subject, let me add there will always be some who will not have as much divine input as others. Because that is true, I believe there will be degrees of eternal punishment. Before you pick up stones to stone me, look closely at these words of Jesus:

> And that slave who knew his master's will and did not get ready or act in accord with his will, shall receive many lashes, but the one who did not know it, and committed deeds worthy of a flogging, will receive but few. And from everyone who has been given much shall much be required; and to whom they entrusted much, of him they will ask all the more (Luke 12:47-48).

Let's understand that no one without Christ spends eternity in heaven. But the *specifics* of how God handles those who are without Christ because they heard so little might very well be answered by this idea of degrees of punishment. But we do know for sure that heaven will not be their home.

3. What about deathbed repentance? This is another gnawing question. I hear about people who turn to the Lord their last day on earth . . . maybe even their last hour. They have spent their entire life apart from faith in the Lord Jesus and now, dying, they express strong and confident faith in the Lord. Is that valid?

Once again remember, no one on earth can determine with absolute certainty the eternal destiny of another individual, since God alone knows the heart. But who is to say no one can become a Christian at the end of his or her life? Remember one of the thieves on the cross? He had lived the life of a criminal, a thief. He had lived his entire life without Christ. But in his final breath he makes a statement regarding eternity, and Christ acknowledges it.

> And one of the criminals who were hanged there was hurling abuse at Him, saying "Are You not the Christ? Save Yourself and us!" But the other answered, and rebuking him said, "Do you not even fear God, since you are under the same sentence of condemnation? And we indeed justly, for we are receiving what we deserve for our deeds; but this man has done nothing wrong." And he was saying, "Jesus, remember me when You come in Your kingdom!" And He said to him, "Truly I say to you, today you shall be with Me in Paradise" (Luke 23:39-43).

There is no doubt in my mind that that thief will spend eternity in heaven.

By the way, we need to be careful about expecting people to say the exact words we want to hear so we can say in return, "Now you're a Christian." Be careful about giving them *the* prayer that they must recite or giving them *the* words that they must repeat. Who can say for sure what language the heart speaks when one "believes in his heart"? I don't think that I've ever heard anyone I have led to the Lord say, "Jesus, remember me when You come in Your kingdom." But in this case that was sufficient. The Lord read the language of his heart. Only He can do that. Yes, deathbed repentance can be sincere and effective.

4. What about the death of babies? This question is extremely important to those who have lost an infant at birth or a little child who never reached an age of spiritual comprehension. It's my understanding that small children who die before reaching a primary level of maturity (when they are able to reason with the basic issues of salvation and faith in the Lord Jesus) go immediately into the presence of the Lord.

No passage of Scripture is any clearer on this subject than 2 Samuel 12:23, where David says of his infant who has just died, ". . . I shall go to him, but he will not return to me." Somehow, in God's wonderful plan, He has reserved in heaven a place for the precious infants and little people whose lives ended prematurely on this earth. David states the truth as he testifies to the inability of his baby to return to earth. But when David himself dies, he will see his child as he enters the presence of the Lord. By the way, the erroneous teaching regarding reincarnation is nullified by David's remark "He will not return to me"—which brings me to my final question.

5. Is reincarnation valid? If you can believe it, I have heard some say that Jesus' words in John 3:8—"You must be born again"—provide a basis for belief in reincarnation. I've also heard Hebrews 12:1 quoted as biblical justification: "We have so great a cloud of witnesses surrounding us ." Proponents of reincarnation say, "See, people have come back, and they now 'surround' us." Quite probably, if there were reincarnation, I think Scripture would clearly refer to several deaths that the same soul passes through. But there is no such occurrence in Scripture. The Bible consistently refers to the death of an individual in the singular. Furthermore, Hebrew 9:27 says, "It is appointed for men to die *once* and after this comes judgment" (emphasis mine). Job's words are also worth noting:

The eye of him who sees me will behold me no more; Thine eyes will be on me, but I will not be (Job 7:8).

And don't forget that "great chasm fixed," which we read about earlier. Luke 16:26 seals the door shut:

And besides, all this, between us and you there is a great chasm fixed, in order that those who wish to come over from here to you may not be able, and that none may cross over from there to us.

When death occurs, a fixed destiny has been determined. The teaching of Scripture denies the possibility of reincarnation.

Now I have one final question for you, which only you can answer.

Where Are *You* Going to Spend Eternity?

Only you can answer that. Read the question once again. I plead with you, do not go on until you have come to terms with this all-important question.

Our country may have been a death-denying culture as recently as the 1960s. What concerns me a great deal more than that is that the majority are still a Christ-rejecting people . . . especially so in these closing years of the twentieth century. But since when do thinking people like you take their cues from the majority? You have certainly read far enough in this book to know what it means to become a Christian. I ask you directly, have you become one?

To be a death-denying individual is not nearly as tragic as being a Christ-rejecting individual. One simply means you'd rather not talk about it, which is fine. The other means you refuse to *believe* it, which could be final. Before you decide to die like that, better remember the "certain rich man" Jesus talked about. While he was alive, he didn't believe either.

He does now.

Major Questions Worth Answering

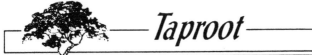

Extending Your Roots

Five major questions are presented in this chapter. They are:

(1) How can a loving God send people to hell?

(2) What about those who have never heard? or, What about those who sincerely follow their own beliefs and their own religion?

(3) What about deathbed repentance?

(4) What about the death of babies?

(5) Is reincarnation valid?

Read each question and answer the question to the best of your knowledge.

2. Now, select one or two questions that you feel need more study. Read the Bible, books, and articles until you can form a personal opinion about the question.

Taproot

Hell is not the eternal dwelling place of a costumed "devil" with red tights, a tail, and a pitchfork. People who choose eternal death will reside in a real place, a horrible place.

1. Using a concordance, look up all verses describing *hell*. Write the descriptions below.

2. Describe in your own words this eternal destiny of the wicked.

3. Place a check mark by your response to these statements.
AGREE   DISAGREE

> God condemns a person to hell.
>
> A person reaps what he sows.
>
> Hell is separation from the presence of God.
>
> The separation from God in hell is final.
>
> There are degrees of punishment in hell.

4. Answer this question: Is hell real to you?

5. How would you explain hell's reality to an unbeliever?

The Return
of Christ

9 | His Coming Is Sure...Are You?

The return of Jesus Christ never fails to create mixed emotions. For those who are ready for it, there is always a sense of comfort and anticipation. For those who are not ready for it (or do not believe in it), there is a mixture of responses. Some are irritated. Some are intimidated. A few are afraid, maybe a little panicked. Most simply refuse to think about it. But no one can remain neutral on the subject.

These thoughts remind me of the true story of what happened to a friend of mine many years ago before he became a Christian. He was hitchhiking his way across the United States. Around dusk one evening, when it looked like rain, he was hoping for a car to pull over before the showers began to fall. Sure enough, a car swerved over to his side of the road, the door flew open, and he heard the driver say, "Hop in." So my friend hopped in, slammed the door, and they took off just as the rain started to fall.

Although daylight was rapidly fading, my friend could just make out the words on a small poster that had been stuck to the dashboard—

WARNING:
IN THE EVENT OF CHRIST'S RETURN
THIS DRIVER WILL DISAPPEAR;
THIS CAR WILL SELF-DESTRUCT

Then in bold, red letters, four final words:

YOU BETTER GIT READY

73

Years later as he was relating the story to me, I asked him how he felt that eerie evening when he read those words. Smiling, he said, "Well, as a matter of fact, it was spooky! I didn't know whether to write my will, to pray, or to jump. But I remember doing two things. First, I kept my door unlocked (as if that were going to help); and second, I engaged the driver in nonstop conversation. I figured he wouldn't suddenly disappear if we kept on talking together."

Isn't it funny how superstitious people can be about future things? And isn't it amazing what decisions people make, thinking that "somehow things will just work out" if they stay close to the right people? It calls to mind the lady who wanted to marry four different men in her lifetime. She said each one would help her with the four things she needed most. First, she wanted to marry a banker. Second, a movie star. Next, a clergyman. And finally, a funeral director. When asked why, she answered, "One for the money, two for the show, three to get ready, and four to go!"

Back to my original story. The driver of the car considered Christ's coming a solid comfort, but the rider viewed it as something spooky . . . a fearful thought. Again, it is almost impossible to remain neutral regarding this future event.

—*Root Issues*—

1. The moviemakers and booksellers of the world throw around lines like "non-stop excitement" or "incredible action" or "gripping narrative." Well, maybe. But compared to 1 Thessalonians 4:13-18, their stuff is about as exciting as reading the telephone book or watching reruns of "Mr. Rogers' Neighborhood." Talk about high drama! Take a walk outside, weather permitting, with your New Testament in hand. Read again this startling glimpse into the future —*your* future. Let your eyes sweep the skies. Feel the thunder, joy, and awe. Remind yourself that this experience

could happen at any moment—even before you return from your walk or draw your next breath. Let your Lord know that you are watching for His return.

2. It's good to contemplate our Lord's sudden descent from heaven—and yet Scripture urges us to do more than stand around staring at the sky. The last words of the Thessalonian passage urge us to "*comfort* one another with these words." The Greek term Paul uses here for "comfort" is translated as "encourage" in 1 Thessalonians 3:2. It's from the Greek terms *Para*, meaning "beside, alongside," and *Kaleo* "to call." *Called alongside*. In one of my earlier books I noted that this implies more than a shallow sympathy card with rhyming words and gold-glitter greeting. It is eternally more than a "slap on the back" or a quick "cheer-up" bit of advice. Paul was writing to a group of people who were enduring intense pressure and persecution for their faith. And he's saying, "Listen, come alongside one another and *encourage* each other with this thought—Jesus is coming back! We'll meet Him—together—in the clouds!" Watch for an opportunity in the coming days to come alongside a struggling fellow believer with the encouragement contained in this passage. When it arrives, comfort!

3. Memorize 1 John 3:2-3. Verse 3 says: "Everyone who has this hope fixed on Him purifies himself, just as He is pure." What does it mean, in a very practical way, for you to live with your hope *fixed* on Him? What impact should the knowledge of His imminent return have on the way you live? Why is this so? Write about these thoughts in your notebook.

4. Why do we usually wait until New Year's Eve—or perhaps after a near brush with death—to soberly weigh the investments of our time, money, and abilities? The truth is, we could find ourselves face to face with our Master *at any moment*. And we should be ready to give an accounting of our activities on His behalf. Consider again the searching truths of the Lord's parable in Luke 19:11-27. Does the story suggest anything to you about the manner in which you are

living your life? Ask the Spirit of God to underline areas where you need to seek change.

5. Do you find the thought of Christ's return a *dread* rather than a *joy* to contemplate? If you do, talk about your feelings with your pastor or a close Christian friend.

Extending Your Roots

1. Jesus used parables as a way of teaching. Some of those parables speak about getting ready for His second coming. Read the two parables below. Use the cross-references in your Bible and a commentary to discover what the parables mean. Write your information in the space provided. Mark 13:32-37

Luke 12:35-48

Taproot

1. Write a brief description of your personal interpretation of the second coming.

Later in our study of the second coming, you will be asked to read your interpretation again and make any changes as a result of new information from this study.

10 | Extremes that Block Our Balance

Fanatical Intensity

Some Christians drop straight off the deep end when prophetic subjects come up. They almost "go nuts" over the subject. When that happens, they seem to lose their practical equilibrium. Such fanatical intensity invariably drives others away as these well-meaning folk overreact to the teaching of prophecy.

Some of the telltale signs? They begin to read prophecy into most newspaper articles, current events, and certainly each major disaster or calamity. They are often surprised that you don't see it as clearly as they do. What's worse, their neurotic intensity creates within them a lack of interest in the here and now. Nothing—absolutely nothing—is more important to them than the then and there. Often, they tend to live rather sheltered and/or irresponsible lives. Some don't mind increasing their indebtedness. After all, their soon departure from Planet Earth provides the perfect escape from financial responsibility! They don't worry too much about today's assignments either because they are so caught up in the tomorrow of God's plan.

The ultimate extremists would be those who set specific dates, then quit their jobs and mooch off others as they wait for the Lord's return.

Many years ago I found a big tract stuck under the windshield wiper on my car. I remember it well. It was one of those four-page, tiny-print jobs. Almost needed a magnifying glass to read the stuff. I can't recall how many dozens of points there were that this person (who happened to be a member of a religious cult) tried to communicate. But his logic was strange and the verses he quoted were twisted and wrenched from their context.

What caught my eye was the date that was set January 31, 1974! Some kind of comet with a blazing tail of fire would bring a "baptism of fire" that would cause a wave of insanity and suicide throughout the earth shortly before Christ returned . . . and we wouldn't be able to escape it if we remained in the United States. We in America needed to be prepared by moving to Canada or Mexico or Puerto Rico or even Hawaii. (It's always safer in Hawaii, it seems.) Everything was sure to end January 31, 1974. Well, on February 1, 1974, I wrote to the address that appeared on the bottom of the tract. I asked a few pointed questions, but I never got an answer. Maybe they were all in Hawaii by then.

Frankly, I call that sort of stuff "prophecy gone to seed." Too much prophetic intensity gets dangerously close to personal insanity.

No matter how much we may love the Lord Jesus Christ and believe in His Word, we need to remember that there is still a life to be lived and responsibilities to be faced. And to cop out because Christ is coming is not only poor practicality, it's abominable theology. Never once in a Scripture is irresponsibility excused on the basis of one's confidence in Christ's return. Anticipation is one thing. Blind fanaticism is quite another.

Theological Ignorance

The other extreme to the far left is theological ignorance. Maybe "personal indifference" would be another way of putting it. The former problem is one of being overinvolved and superintense. But the indifferent individual sees no reason at all to be alert. In fact, he seriously questions that there will be even such a thing as a second coming. A person like that has no interest in evangelism (I have never seen an exception), because there is an absence of urgency. He understands neither God's overall world program nor specifically the imminent (at-any-moment) return of Christ.

There's something about Christ's soon return that stirs up our urgency and keeps us involved. God planned it that way. Anticipating the Savior activates our involvement in today's needs.

C. S. Lewis writes:

> Hope is one of the theological virtues. This means that a continual looking forward to the eternal world is not (as some modern people think) a form of escapism or wishful thinking, but one of the things a Christian is meant to do. It does not mean that we are to leave the present world as it is. If you read history, you will find that the Christians who did most for the present world were just those who thought most of the next. . . . It is since Christians have largely ceased to think of the other world that they have become so ineffective in this. Aim at heaven and you will get earth "thrown in": aim at earth and you will get neither.[1]

Needed Balance

Let's be neither insane nor indifferent about His return. What we need is a balance. We need to be informed and aware, thinking it could occur at any moment, but carrying out our lives as responsibly as if His return would not be for another two or three generations.

In other chapters we have examined Peter's words. Let's look again, this time at his second letter. In this section he writes as an eyewitness of the Lord Jesus. He is building to a climax: the return of the Lord.

> For we did not follow cleverly devised tales when we made known to you the power and coming of our Lord Jesus Christ, but we were eyewitnesses of His majesty. For when He received honor and glory from God the Father, such an utterance as this was made to Him by the Majestic Glory, "This is My beloved Son with whom I am well-pleased"—and we ourselves heard this utterance made from heaven when we were

with Him on the holy mountain. And so we have the prophetic word made more sure, to which you do well to pay attention as to a lamp shining in a dark place, until the day dawns and the morning star arises in your hearts (2 Pet. 1:16-19).

Is that a relevant word? You bet! "I have seen Him. I have heard the voice from heaven. I have listened to His teachings with my own ears and we have a more sure word. You'd do well to listen up."

Next, glance at chapter 3, verses 3 and 4. He writes perhaps to skeptical ears as he says:

> Know this first of all, that in the last days mockers will come with their mocking, following after their own lusts, and saying, "Where is the promise of His coming? For ever since the fathers fell asleep, all continues just as it was from the beginning of creation."

Does that sound like something you heard in your science classes? Did they teach you that in your undergraduate or graduate studies? Probably so. It's called the theory of uniformitarianism. Since the beginning of time to this present day there has been the unfolding, the evolving, of an *uninterrupted* flow of events in history.

"Wrong," says Peter. "They are wrong. They systematically overlook something that intercepted time—the deluge, the universal flood."

> For when they maintain this, it escapes their notice that by the word of God the heavens existed long ago and the earth was formed out of water and by water, through which the world at that time was destroyed, being flooded with water (vv. 5-6).

"They overlook a very important fact," says Peter. "They forget that this earth, as it was created by God and as history was unfolding, was destroyed. They ignore the fact that in the middle of the movement of time, God stepped in and brought a flood. And it caught the attention of everyone on this earth—this deluge." To this day most scholars overlook (or, in some cases explain away) the possibility of a universal flood.

Suddenly, Peter jumps to the future.

> But the present heavens and earth by His word are being reserved for fire, . . . (v. 7a).

In Noah's time, it was destroyed by water. Someday in the future it will be destroyed by fire.

> kept for the day of judgment and destruction of ungodly men. But do not let this one fact escape your notice, beloved, that with the Lord one day is as a thousand years, and a thousand years as one day. The Lord is not slow about His promise, as some count slowness, but is patient toward you, not wishing for any to perish but for all to come to repentance (vv. 7b-9).

The Lord is going to return. We need to "git ready." He doesn't wish for any to perish. I call that clear, specific, and reliable information. When it comes to balance, that says it well. Let's not mistake our Lord's current patience for permanent absence. He *is* coming back.

Extending Your Roots

1. Some Christians overreact when the subject of the second coming is discussed. Scripture does provide numerous signs of the return of the Lord. These signs can be interpreted with fanatical intensity or theological ignorance. Search Matthew 24 for at least eleven signs. List them in the space below.

2. In your opinion, how could these signs be misinterpreted by extremists?

 *Taproot*

1. The interpretations of the predictions and promises of the rapture often cause people to lose their balance about His return. In order to be more informed and aware of this subject, look for the definition of rapture in a dictionary and proceed from there to research the subject as fully as possible. Use reference books and other helps. Determine a balanced way for you to react to the rapture.

2. Think about 1 Corinthians 15:58. Apply this verse to your life in the here and now.

11 Predictions that Affirm Our Assurance

Before looking at other verses of Scripture, let me take you on a brief safari. To begin with, here are some facts about prophecy that will surprise most people:

● One out of every 30 verses in the Bible mentions the subject of Christ's return or the end of time.

● Of the 216 chapters in the New Testament, there are well over 300 references to the return of Jesus Christ.

● Only 4 of the 27 New Testament books fail to mention Christ's return.

● That means one-twentieth of the entire New Testament is dedicated to the subject of our Lord's return.

● In the Old Testament, such well-known and reliable men of God as Job, Moses, David, Isaiah, Jeremiah, Daniel, and most of the minor prophets fixed at least part of their attention on the Lord's return.

● Christ spoke of His return often, especially after He had revealed His death. He never did so in vague or uncertain terms.

● Those who lived on following His teaching, who established the churches and wrote the Scriptures in the first century frequently mentioned His return in their preaching and in their writings.

After those apostles left the earth, the message of Christ's return did not die. On the contrary, it found its way into the Nicene Creed, into the Athanasian Creed, and into the thirty-nine Articles of the Church of England, the fourth of which says, "He ascended into heaven and there sitteth until He returns to judge all men at the last day." The Augsburg Confession deals with it somewhat at length. The familiar Apostles' Creed, repeated at many churches in their liturgy of worship, includes the statement, "from thence He shall come to judge the quick and the dead."

I remember repeating those words as a little boy in a church where our family worshiped. I wondered who "the quick" would be at that time. I understood "the dead." I didn't grasp that *quick* is the Old English term for "living." "He will come to judge the living and the dead."

The Bible teaches it. The Lord Jesus stood upon its truths. The apostles declared it and wrote about it. The creeds include it and affirm it. Quite obviously, His return has not been considered an insignificant issue through the centuries. But the strange thing is that many Christians in this generation either ignore it or are somehow confused by it. Too bad. It is a marvelous truth that only gains significance as we move closer to death.

A few days ago I had a part in the burial of a twenty-one-year-old man who died in an automobile accident. It was a heartrending service. I thought of Christ's return as I looked at the casket. The thought gave me reassuring hope. Only a few days later, one of our longtime church "saints," a godly, one-hundred-year-old woman, passed into the Lord's presence. And when I heard that news, immediately thoughts of Jesus' return flashed through my mind:

> For the Lord Himself will descend from heaven with a shout, with the voice of the archangel, and with the trumpet of God; and the dead in Christ shall rise first. Then we who are alive and remain shall be caught up together with them in the clouds to meet the Lord in the air, and thus we shall always be with the Lord (1 Thess. 4:16-17).

Whether young or old, those who pass into eternity have the same truth to claim . . . and so do those of us who remain. It is something you can cling to when it seems as though all hell has broken loose in your life. When the events of your days seem out of control, having neither rhyme nor reason. Deep within you are reminded that the end has not yet come. When He comes it will all make sense.

Let's take a moment to look briefly at several verses of Scripture that underscore His coming soon.

Matthew 24 is a great place to start. Jesus is speaking:

> Therefore be on the alert, for you do not know which day your Lord is coming. But be sure of this, that if the head of the house had known at what time of the night the thief was coming, he would have been on the alert and would not have allowed his house to be broken into. For this reason you be ready too; for the Son of Man is coming at an hour when you do not think He will (vv. 42-44).
>
> But when the Son of Man comes in His glory, and all the angels with Him, then He will sit on His glorious throne (25:31).

Notice the words "when" and "will"—not "if" but "when" —not "may" but "will." There was no question in Jesus' mind.

From Matthew 25, turn to Mark, chapter 8.

> For whoever wishes to save his life shall lose it; but whoever loses his life for My sake and the gospel's sake shall save it. For what does it profit a man to gain the whole world, and forfeit his soul? For what shall a man give in exchange for his soul? For whoever is ashamed of Me and My words in this adulterous and sinful generation, the Son of Man will also be ashamed of him when He comes in the glory of His Father with the holy angels (vv. 35-38).

This kind of teaching must have stunned the disciples. They had anticipated the establishment of Jesus' earthly kingdom then and there. They expected it to be in motion before the end of their generation, when Jesus would be ruling as King of kings and Lord of lords. They envisioned themselves as charter members in His kingdom band. With great delight they would witness the overthrow of Rome and Israel's numerous enemies. What a hope!

But then one dark night in a second-story flat, along some

street in the city of Jerusalem, Jesus ate His last meal with them. There, he unfolded the startling truth that His death was only hours away. They must have wanted to stop their ears from hearing Him say, "I'm going to leave you. I'm going back to My Father."

Looking into the eyes of those disillusioned men who must have felt a bit orphaned, Jesus said:

> Let not your heart be troubled; believe in God, believe also in Me. In My Father's house are many dwelling places; if it were not so, I would have told you; for I go to prepare a place for you (John 14:1-2).

It is very important that you understand heaven, our eternal destiny, is an *actual place*. It isn't a misty dream or a floating fantasy. Don't let any of the mystical religions confuse you. Heaven is reality. Literal real estate which He is preparing for His own. Jesus says so in the next statement.

> And if I go and prepare a place for you, I will come again, and receive you to Myself; that where I am, there you may be also (v. 3).

The body of every believer that now resides in a casket, every believer torn apart by ravenous beasts or by the elements of the sea or by warfare or awful murder will be received by the Christ at His return. Regardless of the condition of that body, the Lord Jesus says, "I *will* come again, and I *will* receive you unto Myself." That's a direct promise from His lips. Most of those men who heard His words that evening died horrible deaths. More than one of them were sawn in two. Some were torn apart by wild beasts. Yet their Lord said, in effect, "I will come again, and I'll receive you unto Myself. The condition of your body doesn't concern Me. This promise stands firm."

Shortly thereafter Jesus went to the cross. When He died He was placed in a tomb. Three days later, He emerged in bodily form from the tomb, victorious over death. He is the only one thus far who has ever been resurrected—the only one to come back to this earth in a glorified condition. So He has overcome death. In light of that, it shouldn't surprise us that He is able to bring us from the grave when He returns.

Forty days after His resurrection He stood on a mountain with His followers. While there, just before He ascended to heaven, the subject of His return was brought up again.

> And so when they had come together, they were asking Him, saying, "Lord, is it at this time You are restoring the kingdom to Israel?" He said to them, "It is not for you to know times or epochs which the Father has fixed by His own authority; but you shall receive power when the Holy Spirit has come upon you, and you shall be My witnesses both in Jerusalem, and in all Judea and Samaria, and even to the remotest part of the earth." And after He had said these things, He was lifted up while they were looking on, and a cloud received Him out of their sight (Acts 1:6-9).

Wow! Can you *imagine* that moment? As they watched, Jesus was lifted up out of sight. We think we're pretty hot stuff because we can put people in a rocket, send them into an orbit around the earth a few times, then bring them back. Yet with no physical assistance, with nothing around Him or near Him, He was lifted up from the earth —whoosh!—and went directly through the clouds back to heaven. His followers did just what you and I would have done—they stood with mouths open, gazing intently into the skies.

> And as they were gazing intently into the sky while He was departing, behold, two men in white clothing stood beside them; and they also said, "Men of Galilee, . . ." (vv. 10-11a).

I want to write the following words to people who are pre-occupied with Christ's return, spending most of their time looking up, as if they had nothing else to do—

> "Why do you stand looking into the sky? This Jesus, who has been taken up from you into heaven, will come in just the same way as you have watched Him go into heaven."

He is coming back. Looking up won't bring Him any sooner.

We're never told simply to stand around gazing up to heaven. In fact, we're told *not* to do that. We aren't even commanded to do a lot of talking about it. There's a bigger job to be done than sitting around discussing the details of His return!

In the last book of the Bible, Revelation, Jesus is being quoted by John who writes these last words:

> I, Jesus, have sent My angel to testify to you these things for the churches. I am the root and the offspring of David, the bright morning star. . . . He who testifies to these things says, "Yes, I am coming quickly." Amen. Come, Lord Jesus (22:16, 20).

Extending Your Roots

1. One prediction that affirms our assurance of Jesus' return is found in Revelation 22. Read verses 12-14. Notice that when Jesus comes, He will bring His reward (v. 12). On what basis will the reward be given to people?

2. The word "blessed" in verse 14 means happy. What is there about the second coming of Christ that can cause a Christian to be happy?

Taproot

1. Read Acts 1:6-11. Listed below are some familiar ministries practiced by most churches and Christians. Beside

each ministry, write a *specific* plan for accomplishing that ministry until Jesus returns.

evangelism:

stewardship:

worship:

prayer:

outreach:

Bible study:

missions:

other:

Warning: Don't spend most of your adult Christian life looking up as if you had nothing else to do.

12 Scriptures that Describe Our Destiny

So much for a general overview. There are two passages that are worth turning back to and getting a little closer focus on. First Corinthians 15:50-58 is the first and 1 Thessalonians 4:13-18 is the second. Both of these Scriptures describe our destiny. The Corinthian passage emphasizes the *changes* that will come over us when Christ returns for His own. The Thessalonian passage emphasizes the *order of events* that will occur in the future.

First Corinthians 15:50-58

After developing a thorough statement on resurrection, the apostle Paul presents a tradition in verse 50.

> Now I say this, brethren, that flesh and blood cannot inherit the kingdom of God; nor does the perishable inherit the imperishable.

Understand what he means. He is talking to those of us who are earthlings, people who have been earthbound all our lives. We are people in the process of dying. How many of us in our fifties can remember our younger days when we were in our twenties? We felt different and we certainly looked different. Now there are physical signs on our bodies that mark us as aging people. We all have loved ones in their seventies and eighties, maybe even their nineties, who certainly reveal "perishable" mortality. In order for these bodies of ours to last throughout eternity in what is here called "the kingdom of God," *there must be a change* so that our

91

bodies are made ageless. There must be some kind of molecular reconstruction within us that prepares us for eternity. Our bodies must be changed into a glorified state. All these changes will equip our bodies to last eternally. Since our future will be a bodily existence in heaven, we must undergo bodily changes. Remember now, our eternal existence is not simply spirit existence, but bodily existence. So Paul emphasizes our future changes in the next three verses:

> Behold, I tell you a mystery; we shall not all sleep, but *we shall all be changed*, in a moment, in the twinkling of an eye, at the last trumpet; for the trumpet will sound, and the dead will be raised imperishable, and *we shall be changed*. For this perishable must put on the imperishable, and this mortal must put on immortality (vv. 51-53, emphasis mine).

Paul calls this revelation "a mystery." In our day, a *mystery* suggests something that is complicated, like a riddle, hard to unravel and difficult to solve—complex. But a mystery (*musterion*) in Paul's day was not something that was complex, but something that was more like our word *secret*. It's like he was writing, "Listen, I want to tell you a secret." There's a difference. Once someone tells you a secret, it isn't complicated. All you need is the information.

Here's the thought: "Behold, I want to reveal something that has been a secret up to now—something you will find mentioned nowhere else in God's revelation prior to this revelation." What is that secret? Namely this: There will be a generation alive at the time Christ comes back . . . and those living believers, at the time Christ returns, will be instantly changed and taken back to be with Him forever. Not only will the dead be raised and changed, but those believers who are alive will also be changed.

> But when this perishable will have put on the imperishable, and this mortal will have put on immortality, then will come about the saying that is written, "Death is swallowed up in victory. O death, where is your victory? O death, where is your sting?" (vv. 54-55).

Paul didn't get that from Shakespeare; Shakespeare got

that from Paul! Death will have won its final victory. When we are taken up, the grim reaper will hang up his scythe. Finally, at long last, death will bite the dust. Up to now it may seem he is king. Death visits every home. He steps into the life of every person who has ever lived. No matter how great or how cruel, how good or how bad, death comes. And as he is often pictured, the grim reaper cuts everyone down to size. Euripides the poet was right, "Death is the debt we all must pay." But the marvelous good news is that when our final change at Christ's coming occurs, death will never again have charge of us. At that glorious moment we shall begin a timeless, ageless existence. For the next few moments, meditate on the closing words in this chapter.

> The sting of death is sin, and the power of sin is the law; but thanks be to God, who gives us the victory through our Lord Jesus Christ. Therefore, my beloved brethren, be steadfast, immovable, always abounding in the work of the Lord, knowing that your toil is not in vain in the Lord (vv. 56-58).

How often I quote these words to myself!

First Thessalonians 4:13-18

Remember now, we have nothing to worry about regarding the condition of the body when death occurs. *We shall be changed.* The One who made our bodies from nothing will have no difficulty making us again, even from little bits and pieces if necessary. He'll be able to put us all together.

Let me point out four observations from this passage.

We Are to Be Informed

> But we do not want you to be uninformed, brethren, about those who are asleep (v. 13*a*).

As I have said all along, ignorance is not bliss. The Lord doesn't smile on us when, as we think about the future, we say, "Well, actually, nobody can know for sure. We just hope things work out all right." That's an ignorance and incorrect response. He *wants* us to be informed and knowledgeable. We are to know what's in front of us—at least the broad brush strokes of His plan. Knowing the future gives us confidence in the present.

We Are Not to Grieve as Those Without Hope

that you may not grieve, as do the rest who have no hope (v. 13*b*).

Death brings sorrow. Sorrow brings tears. Tears are part of the grieving process. God never tells us, "Don't cry. Don't grieve." He says we are not to grieve *as those who have no hope.* I am saddened when I see parents, well-meaning though they may be, who correct their children for crying because a loved one dies. Crying is the most natural response when we lose someone or something important to us. We have every reason to grieve and to be sad, but our grief is not as the hopeless when they grieve. You see, we have an answer beyond the grave. They do not. It is this hope that ultimately brings comfort.

We Are to Face Death Without Fear

For if we believe that Jesus died and rose again, even so God will bring with Him those who have fallen asleep in Jesus (v. 14).

Now the reason Christ's own resurrection is so important is because we can anticipate rising as He did. Had He not come back from beyond, we couldn't expect to either. I often think of the followers of some guru. They die. They look next to them in the grave and—there's their guru! Their great spiritual leader. He's still there. If he didn't get out himself, then I ask you how is he going to get *them* out? But no one will ever see a dead Jesus. Why? He has been raised. He has gone beyond the grave. His tomb is empty. Because He died and rose again He is able to give us an answer to sin, death, and the grave. If we believe in Him, then we are ready to be taken with Him. He will bring us along with all those who have fallen asleep in Jesus. Because He lives, all fear is gone!

We Are to Know the Order of Events

> For this we say to you by the word of the Lord, that we who are alive, and remain until the coming of the Lord, shall not precede those who have fallen asleep. For the Lord Himself will descend from heaven with a shout, with the voice of the archangel, and with the trumpet of God; and the dead in Christ shall rise first. Then we who are alive and remain shall be caught up together with them in the clouds to meet the Lord in the air, and thus we shall always be with the Lord (vv. 15-17).

Here is the overall order of events: "The Lord Himself will descend from heaven." That's *first*. I like the way Phillips renders it:

> One word of command, one shout from the archangel, one blast from the trumpet of God.

Imagine the scene! Perhaps all those things will come simultaneously . . . in one great voice, one grand sound. I smile as I write these words. They never fail to excite me!

Next, "the dead in Christ shall rise first."

Then, "we who are alive and remain shall be caught up together with them. . . ."

With whom? The dead who have been changed, who have been raised ahead of us.

Finally, we—

> shall be caught up together with them in the clouds to meet the Lord in the air, and thus we shall always be with the Lord (v. 17*b*).

It is my personal conviction that our Lord Jesus will come for us in the sky—in the clouds. Following that reunion in the air, there will occur on this earth a time of awful judgment, a time of unrestrained pain and great tribulation, following which our Savior will return to this earth and establish the fulfillment of His millennial promises to Israel, a literal one-thousand-year reign over this earth as He serves as King of kings and Lord of lords. My personal belief is that the return of the Lord Jesus for His own, as described in

Thessalonians and in Corinthians, is *prior* to that awful time of tribulation on the earth and *prior* to His establishment of a literal kingdom on earth over which He reigns as King.

This pegs me as a pretribulational premillenialist! But don't let all that make you nervous. I still have great fellowship with those in other camps. Not everybody does, however. I heard about a guy who was so premillennial he wouldn't even eat Post Toasties!

Now the most important thing for you to understand is that *He is coming again.* And, secondly, that *it is a comfort to you* because you have believed in Him. Be sure that the one you believe in has conquered death, otherwise he won't get you into heaven. Hell awaits you. The only way to get beyond the grave and into the Lord's presence is to place your trust on One who has gone before you and has paved the way.

Extending Your Roots

Read 1 Thessalonians 4:13-18. Four observations from this passage need our focus.

1. Read again verse 13. Write one thing you can know for sure about the future.

2. What does Paul mean by "no hope"? Refer to Paul's brief discussion of the doctrine of the second coming of Christ in Titus 2:11-15.

3. Read verse 14 in a paraphrase. Are there any unanswered questions you have about death?

4. Write the name of a person you would feel comfortable about asking for help with this subject.

5. The order of events for the second coming are found in verses 1 Thessalonians 4:15-17. Arrange the events in proper order:

_____ Great musical fanfare from a trumpet.

_____ Christ will return visibly with a mighty shout.

_____ Believers who are alive will be lifted into the clouds to meet Christ.

_____ A shout from an angel.

_____ Believers in Christ who are dead will rise from their graves.

Plan to study more about this great doctrine in the future. Set a time for your study today.

Taproot

Although Christians disagree about how Jesus will return, all agree that He *will* return. As we discussed, views about how Jesus will return and what will happen are subject to different interpretations. The three major views among most Christians concerning the millennium are amillennialism, premillennialism (historical or dispensational), and postmillennialism. Faithful Christians may be found holding any of these views.

Amillennialists believe that Christ's second coming will conclude the history of mankind and that eternity will then begin. Christians and unbelievers will enter into their respective destinies, heaven and hell. Amillennialists do not believe in a literal thousand-year reign of Christ and the saints on earth. The word *amillennialism* simply means no millennium.

Postmillennialists believe that through the work of Christians, the gospel will triumph over the forces of evil on earth. After the victory, Christ will return to set up His kingdom.

Historical premillennialism is so named because those who hold this view consider it to represent the historic view of the church down through the ages about the premillennial coming of Christ. According to this view, Christ will return to the earth to reign for a thousand years over all who have trusted Him by faith, including Gentile and Jewish Christians.

Dispensational premillennialism, in contrast to historical premillennialism, emphasizes the place of the nation of Israel. According to this view, Christ will return to the earth to reign for a literal thousand years, during which time the Old Testament promises to Israel will be fulfilled. The church will be with Christ in the heavenly Jerusalem.

Be assured that God is in control and Jesus is coming back. As a believer, you will be victorious over all forms of evil. As Christians, you can celebrate His victory every day of your life.

13 Actions that Reveal Our Readiness

How do we know if we are prepared for Christ's return? I think there are at least three ways we can reveal our readiness.

First, we continue to walk by faith. Rather than walking by sight and shaping our lives on the basis of the visible, we walk by faith.

Second, we continue to live in peace. We view the present and our future not with panic but with peace. We don't live worried, hassled lives.

And *third*, we rely on hope. The hope that gets me through the tests on this earth is the same hope that will get me through the grave at death, because the One in whom I have believed has gone before me. He is preparing a place for me. He is the embodiment of my hope. Because He lives, we shall live also. The secret of escape from the prison of this body and the pain of this planet is knowing the One who can guarantee our getting beyond the grave.

An old "Alfred Hitchcock" TV episode showed the flip side to this sure and certain hope. As you might expect, the point was made in a rather chilling way.

There was this rather wicked, two-faced woman who murdered an individual. And though she had often done wrong on previous occasions and had always gotten away with it, the court found her guilty in this case, and the judge sentenced her to life in prison. Even though she screamed in the judge's face and announced that she would escape from any prison they put her in, they sent her away.

She took that infamous bus ride to the prison. En route,

she noticed something that became part of her escape plan. She saw an old man, an inmate, covering up a grave outside the prison walls. She realized the only way to get out of the prison was to know someone who had the key to the gate. The only one who did was the old man who assisted in the burial of those who died within the walls. Actually, he built the caskets as well as placed the remains in each casket. His job included rolling the casket on an old cart to the grave site outside the wall and then lowering it into the hole and covering it up with dirt.

The old man was going blind. He needed cataract surgery, but he had no money to pay for it. She told him that it would be worth his while if he would help her escape.

"No ma'am, I can't do that."

"Oh, yes you can," she insisted. "I have all the money you need outside these walls to pay for your cataract surgery. And if you hope to have that operation, then you help me out of this place."

He reluctantly agreed.

Here was the plan: The next time she heard the toll of the bell, which signaled the death of an inmate, she would slip down to his workroom where he made the caskets. She was to locate the casket in which the old man had placed the corpse and then (if you can imagine!) secretly slide herself into that same casket and pull the top down tightly. Early the next morning the old man would roll her, along with the corpse in the casket, out to the place of burial, drop it into the hole, and dump the dirt on it. The next day he was to come back, uncover the grave, pry the top loose, and set her free. Perfect plan. Almost.

Late one night she heard the deep toll of the bell . . . someone had died. This was her moment! She secretly slid off her cot, made her way down an eerie hallway, and, looking into the dimly lit room, she saw the casket. Without hesitation, she lifted the lid and in the darkness slipped into the box and, after squeezing in beside the corpse, she pulled the lid down tightly.

Within a matter of hours she could feel the wheels rolling

Actions that Reveal Our Readiness

as they were making their way to the grave site. She smiled as the casket was placed in the hole. She began to hear the clumps of dirt as they hit the top of the casket. Before long, she was sealed beneath the earth—still smiling!

Silence followed. She could hardly contain her excitement. Time began to drag. The next day came and passed into the night without the old man showing up. But now she has broken into a cold sweat. "Where was he? What could possibly have gone wrong? Why hadn't he shown up?"

In a moment of panic she lights a match and glances at the corpse next to her. You guessed it—*it is the old man himself* who had died!

Slowly, the camera lifts from the grave site, and all you can hear is the hollow, wailing cry of the woman who will never get out of the grave.

I thought of the proverb, "There is a way that seems right unto a man, but the end thereof are the ways of death." She thought she could escape death's jaws, but the one in whom she had placed her hopes was, himself, a victim of the very thing she dreaded most. She trusted in the wrong man.

One day Jesus Christ will come for us. His coming is sure, and He will keep His promise. Since He has conquered death, He will get us beyond those jaws as well.

If you are ready, the thought of His coming is a comfort. If not, it's a dread. The secret of escape is being sure you know the One who can get us out of the grave. His coming is sure— are you?

Extending Your Roots

When we are ready for the second coming of our Lord Jesus Christ, we reveal our readiness in the way we live, day by day, day by day, day by day. Three evidences of our readiness are we walk by faith; live in peace; and rely on hope.

Growing Deep in the Christian Life: Eternity

1. Select one day next week for keeping a record of evidences of your readiness. Use the space below for writing about your day.

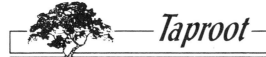 *Taproot*

1. Turn back to the Taproot in chapter 9. What new things have you learned about Christ's second coming?

2. How have your thoughts about this event changed?

3. How will you live differently this week because you know His coming is sure?

14 Until He Returns. . . What?

The books in the *Growing Deep in the Christian Life* study series are the major doctrines taught in the Bible. As I have written or implied all along, these aren't theoretical, exhaustive textbooks but practical guides to help people focus on and think through their faith. This approach allows me the wobble room I need to deal with sideline issues that relate to a doctrine, though they do not necessarily fall into a major doctrinal category.

In other books in this series, for example, we have not only thought about the doctrine of the Bible, but also the importance of discernment as we study the Bible and the value of handling the Bible with accuracy. Furthermore, we not only thought through Jesus' virgin birth and incarnation, but we took the time to see how He impacts and changes lives. To me, those practical issues are too significant to leave unsaid. Each doctrine has a practical side we dare not overlook.

We have investigated the scriptural evidence of Christ's return . . . not in great detail, but sufficiently to realize that He is indeed coming back. As I mentioned earlier, we cannot ignore the fact that, while His return is sure, He may not return in this generation—or even the next. So what do we do in the meantime? That question may not be a major doctrine but it certainly is a major issue. The late Francis Schaeffer asked the right question, "How Should We Then Live?" What ought to occupy our time? What do we do between now and when He returns?

There once lived a farmer named William Miller. It was

back in the nineteenth century. Miller began a religion. One of the marks of his religion was an intense belief in Christ's return. He was notorious for setting dates. He and his followers (known as the Millerites) often met for camp meetings. During one of these meetings, a date was set for the Lord's return. The Millerites decided to pull together and rally around the prediction regardless of public reaction.

The date was announced: Jesus would return between March 21, 1842, and March 21, 1843. During that year they were to ready themselves for Christ's arrival. He was sure to return! To make a yearlong story short, He didn't. Disappointment swept through the Millerite ranks, though Miller himself was undaunted. He had simply "miscalculated." So he sharpened his pencil, refigured the details, and set another date. This time Jesus would *definitely* return. The announcement was made on August 12, 1844: He would come between October 20 and October 22, 1844. "Get ready for the end of the world."

As time drew very near, a sign was displayed on a Philadelphia store window:

THIS SHOP WILL BE CLOSED
IN HONOR OF THE
KING OF KINGS WHO WILL APPEAR
ABOUT THE
TWENTIETH OF OCTOBER.
GET READY, FRIENDS,
TO CROWN HIM LORD OF ALL.

A group of about two hundred Millerites sold or gave away their possessions (I've often wondered why they sold their things if they were sure the world was going to end) and prepared their wardrobe for the soon-coming King. They gathered and waited in white robes for His coming. And waited. And waited. And waited. October 20 came and went. So did the 21st and the 22nd, and, of course, the 23rd. Five years later, William Miller died. I think the wisest statement that was ever made by the Millerites was put on his tombstone. It reads, "At the appointed time the end shall be." Finally, they demonstrated good theology! Not on March 21, 1842, or on October 20, 1844. Not on July 7, 1909, or on November 25, 1947, nor even the first day of the year 2001, but *at the appointed time* the end shall be.

Extending Your Roots

1. Since we can be absolutely sure of the return of Christ, we should be motivated to godly, holy living. Certain evidences of this kind of living will be seen by others. The following list suggests what our life-style should proclaim to others.

Read the list and think about Bible people who gave evidence of godly, holy living. You may want to plan a biographical study of one or more of these individuals at a later time.

- Committed to the choice of God's will
- Ministering to others in Jesus' name
- Appreciative of spiritual values
- Controlled by what is right. Diligent to defeat wrong.
- Guided by Christian love.
- Displays the fruit of the Holy Spirit.
- Loyal to Christ and the church.

Taproot

Of course "What if" questions surface concerning the return of Jesus. Pretend you are a well-informed Bible student about the subject of the second coming. How would you respond to these individuals or groups?

1. WHAT IF I go ahead and plan for college, arrange for a student loan, take the entrance tests, and Jesus returns during my junior year? Won't those years of education and money be wasted?

1. WHAT IF we go ahead and open long-term savings accounts? Isn't it silly to save money we could be enjoying now?

3. WHAT IF we do relocate our church to a new and larger area and Jesus comes before we finish the project? Don't you think it is wiser to stay put and wait and see if He returns?

4. WHAT IF I study all about the second coming and find out that Jesus isn't coming back to earth? What then?

5. WHAT IF I just go ahead and live my life like I want too. I can make the right changes before Jesus comes. Look how long it has already been.

6. Do you have any personal WHAT IFS?

What advice would you give to yourself?

15 The Appointed Time

His coming is sure, but it may not be when you think it's going to be. It may not even be as soon as you think it will be. Chances are good it will be sooner than many anticipate. But, again I repeat, no one can say when. To put it bluntly, date-setters are out to lunch. Always have been . . . always will be! No one knows for sure. But there are a couple of things we *do* know. We can be sure of both.

Historically

We are sure that Christ will return. As we saw in the previous chapter, that fact is well-documented. Look at Matthew, chapter 24, for example.

> Heaven and earth will pass away, but My words shall not pass away. But of that day and hour no one knows, not even the angels of heaven, nor the Son, but the Father alone. For the coming of the Son of Man will be just like the days of Noah. For as in those days which were before the flood they were eating and drinking, they were marrying and giving in marriage (vv. 35-38*a*).

The picture Jesus is painting is a normal life-style. Before the flood in Noah's day, some people were working; others were sleeping. Some were being born, while others were marrying. People were dying. It was a normal, everyday life-style.

> until the day that Noah entered the ark, and they did not understand until the flood came and took them all away, so shall the coming of the Son of Man be. Then there shall be two men in the field; one will be taken, and one will be left.

The Appointed Time

Two women will be grinding at the mill; one will be taken, and one will be left. Therefore be on the alert, for you do not know which day your Lord is coming (vv. 38*b*-42).

Now the point here is rather obvious. We do not know the exact time, but we are absolutely sure of the fact. He *is* coming again. It will occur when life on earth is rolling along.

Now before we consider the second thing we know for sure, let's listen to the words of a reputable student of prophecy:

> A short time ago, I took occasion to go through the New Testament to mark each reference to the coming of the Lord Jesus Christ and to observe the use made of that teaching about His coming. I was struck anew with the fact that almost without exception, when the coming of Christ is mentioned in the New Testament, it is followed by an exhortation to godliness and holy living. While the study of prophecy will give us proof of the authority of the Word of God, will reveal the purpose of God and the power of God, and will give us the peace and assurance of God, we have missed the whole purpose of the study of prophecy if it does not conform us to the Lord Jesus Christ in our daily living.[1]

You see, God never intended the truth of His Son's return simply to stir up our curiosity or to give us the big-time tingles. God has given us the truth concerning His Son's return to prompt holy living. We study the prophetic word so we can keep our act cleaned up, so that we will be ready at any moment and will not be embarrassed to meet Him face to face. You may remember that on the heels of that great New Testament chapter on resurrection and Jesus' return, 1 Corinthians 15, the final verse exhorts us to stay at the tasks of responsible living.

> Therefore, my dear brothers, stand firm. Let nothing move you. Always give yourselves fully to the work of the Lord, because you know that your labor in the Lord is not in vain (v. 58, NIV).

Prophetically

We also know this: Nothing stands in the way of Christ's return. That is why I have repeatedly used the term *imminent* . . . Jesus' coming could occur at any moment. In other words, there is no future event in God's timetable that must take place before Christ comes in the clouds for His own. Nothing! Candidly, I find that rather exciting. Since we know for sure He's coming, yet we don't know for sure when . . . any day or any hour could be the one!

H. L. Turner was right, over a hundred years ago, when he wrote:

> It may be at morn, when the day is awaking,
> When sunlight through darkness and shadow is breaking,
> That Jesus will come in the fullness of glory,
> To receive from the world His own.
>
> O joy! O delight! should we go without dying,
> No sickness, no sadness, no dread and no crying,
> Caught up through the clouds with our Lord into glory,
> When Jesus receives His own.[2]

My maternal grandfather, whom I loved dearly, used to say that he looked forward to dying because he wanted to go through the whole process as a Christian. Rather than by-passing death, he wanted to go through it. He wanted to know in a conscious manner, the joy of life beyond the grave. He wanted to experience his body's bursting out of the ground, glorified and fitted for eternity, brought immediately into the Lord's presence. As I recall, he used to say that those who were going to be taken up while they are alive are only getting part of the blessing. But those who go through the whole death process "are going to get their money's worth!" In fact, they get preferential treatment. As we saw earlier, we will not precede those who have fallen asleep. They will be raised first, and then we will be brought up with them, glorified, to meet the Lord in the air.

Well, dear, old L. O. Lundy got his wish. He has died and

his body awaits the Savior's arrival. Any day now he's going to get his "money's worth."

What if He doesn't return in this generation? What if that little family you're beginning to raise grows up and you grow old, still waiting for the Lord's return? What if you become a grandparent or a great-grandparent in the distant years of the future, and He still hasn't come back? How are we to conduct ourselves? What does the Bible teach about life during the interlude? We'll answer that question in the last chapter of our study.

Extending Your Roots

1. Personal purity is important to an individual who is preparing for the second coming of Christ. Using a Bible concordance, read all the Scripture passages listed under the words *pure* or *purity*. Record your discoveries.

2. Focus on Jesus' prayer in John 17. Read verse 17 aloud. Jesus wants His followers to be pure. How does this come about?

3. Consider making a contract with yourself as you prepare for Christ's return. Fill in the following contract after praying and as you feel led by God.

Growing Deep in the Christian Life: Eternity

Purity Contract

I, _____, agree with myself to prepare for the return of Christ, by staying as personally pure as I know how. I will practice a life-style that leads to a godly, holy life.

As I seek to do this, I will be:

I will seek to do:

I will not:

Date:

Signature:_____

Now put your contract away and begin the preparation.

Taproot

An ordinance is a prescribed practice given by authoritative decree or direction. In church life, it is a specific practice instituted and commanded by God.

1. Have you ever thought about the Lord's Supper being something we do while we wait for the return of Christ. Read 1 Corinthians 11:23-28.

2. According to Scripture, why should a self-examination precede participation in the Lord's Supper?

The Appointed Time

3. Recall a Lord's Supper experience that was especially meaningful to you and describe it. Did the experience make you think about the second coming?

4. Plan to participate in the next observance of the Lord's Supper at your church.

16 But . . . in the Meantime

There are four words I want you to remember. You might even want to commit them to memory. These four words represent God's "marching orders" for us—our in-the-meantime standard operating procedure:

- Occupy
- Purify
- Watch
- Worship

If someone asks you, "What are we supposed to do before Christ comes? What is our involvement? Our commitment?" these four words will provide an answer. They are not only wise words of practical counsel, all four are taught in the Scripture. Let's examine each one in greater detail.

Occupy

Dr. Luke records a parable Jesus taught in which He addressed the importance of life continuing on until the Lord returns. Take the time to read the entire account.

> And while they were listening to these things, He went on to tell a parable, because He was near Jerusalem, and they supposed that the kingdom of God was going to appear immediately. He said therefore, "A certain nobleman went to a distant country to receive a kingdom for himself, and then return. And he called ten of his slaves, and gave them ten minas, and said to them, 'Do business with this until I come back.' But his citizens hated him, and sent a delegation after him, saying, 'We do not want this man to reign over us.' And it came about that when he returned, after receiving the

kingdom, he ordered that these slaves, to whom he had given the money, be called to him in order that he might know what business they had done. And the first appeared, saying, 'Master, your mina has made ten minas more.' And he said to him, 'Well done, good slave, because you have been faithful in a very little thing, be in authority over ten cities.' And the second came, saying, "Your mina, master, has made five minas." And he said to him also, 'And you are to be over five cities.' And another came, saying, 'Master, behold your mina, which I kept put away in a handkerchief; for I was afraid of you, because you are an exacting man; you take up what you did not lay down, and reap what you did not sow.' He said to him. 'By your own words I will judge you, you worthless slave. Did you know that I am an exacting man, taking up what I did not lay down, and reaping what I did not sow? Then why did you not put the money in the bank, and having come, I would have collected it with interest?' And he said to the bystanders, 'Take the mina away from him, and give it to the one who has the ten minas.' And they said to him, 'Master, he has ten minas already.' 'I tell you, that to everyone who has shall more be given, but from the one who does not have, even what he does have shall be taken away. But these enemies of mine, who did not want me to reign over them, bring them here, and slay them in my presence' " (Luke 19:11-27).

A "mina" was a lot of money, in fact about a hundred day's wages (nearly twenty dollars in those days). The nobleman gave his slaves ten of those coins as he instructed all of them to "do business" while he was away.

You may wish to circle the words "do business." More than one version of Scripture renders the same command "occupy." "Do business," however, is a good way of saying it. The point is clear. It was the nobleman's desire that his servants not sit back, doing nothing—letting his money collect dust—until he returned. But they failed to do as he had commanded.

Finally, he returned. Immediately the nobleman was interested in their activity while he had been away. The report was anything but pleasing. Except for the first one who had multiplied his investment tenfold and the second one fivefold, the slaves had failed to "occupy" during his absence.

The lessons from this story are numerous, but it is noteworthy that the nobleman (Jesus) smiled upon the wise use of money during the interlude. He was pleased with the investments of those who made much of the goods of this earth. That's part of doing business. To put it in different words, we "occupy" when we live responsibly, work diligently, plan wisely, think realistically, invest carefully. In neither the Old nor New Testament is laziness smiled upon, especially laziness that is rationalized because one believes in the soon-coming of Christ. Our Lord frowns on the lack of discipline and diligence. He smiles on a well-ordered private life. He is pleased with the wise use of our time and the proper handling of our possessions. Some excuse irresponsibility by giving it a spiritual-sounding title, like "walking by faith" or "trusting the Lord." Let's not tempt the Lord with such rationalization.

There once lived a group of Christians who bought into that mentality. They thought that since they knew Christ was coming and since their teacher, the apostle Paul himself, had assured them that the Lord was coming soon, why work? Why even concern themselves with the mundane details of everyday life? They'd just spend their days awaiting His coming. And until He arrived they would live off of others. If others chose to work, fine; but they would be the ones who "lived by faith." Once Paul heard of that, he jumped on it like a hen on a June bug:

> Now we command you, brethren, in the name of our Lord Jesus Christ, that you keep aloof from every brother who leads an unruly life and not according to the tradition which you received from us. For you yourselves know how you ought to follow our example, because we did not act in an undisciplined manner among you, nor did we eat anyone's bread without paying for it, but with labor and hardship we kept working night and day so that we might not be a burden to any of you; not because we do not have the right to this,

but in order to offer ourselves as a model for you, that you might follow our example. For even when we were with you, we used to give you this order: if anyone will not work, neither let him eat. For we hear that some among you are leading an undisciplined life, doing no work at all, but acting like busybodies (2 Thess. 3:6-12).

Honestly, doesn't a part of that sound like your dad's counsel? I can just hear my father's voice in those words! Especially, "If someone will not work, neither let him eat." But this is more than a father's advice . . . these are words from the authoritative Scripture. Those who have a right to eat are those who work. Even though we believe strongly in Christ's soon return, and even though we claim to be walking by faith, if we plan to eat while waiting, working is God's plan for us.

Then this final admonition:

But as for you, brethren, do not grow weary of doing good. And if anyone does not obey our instruction in this letter, take special note of that man and do not associate with him, so that he may be put to shame (vv. 13-14).

I call that straight talk—hard talk.

Every once in a while we meet up with some dear soul with eyes at half-mast, who wants to sit on a hill, strum a guitar, eat birdseed, and sing Christian folk tunes. His (or her) idea of the faith-life is just gathering dew and watching the weeds and daisies grow up all around. This Scripture strikes at the heart of such thinking. God has limited patience with people who irresponsibly hide behind "faith" as they leave it to others to pay their bills.

And to make matters worse, they say the reason they're doing that is because they really love the Lord Jesus. No, more often than not the reason they do that is because they are lazy. For them, the soon-coming of Christ is a wonderful cop-out. The next time one of them attempts to quote verses to support their rationalization, I suggest you counter with 2 Thessalonians 3:10—"If anyonewill not work, neither let him eat."

So much for "occupy." Get a job. Work hard. Think realistically. Plan ahead. Reorder your private world. Get your act together. Live responsibly. Invest carefully.

Our Lord expects nothing less.

Purify

There is a second word to remember while we're in the process of preparing for His coming— purify. I find biblical support for this in Titus 2:11-14:

> For the grace of God has appeared, bringing salvation to all men, instructing us to deny ungodliness and worldly desires and to live sensibly, righteously and godly in the present age, looking for the blessed hope and the appearing of the glory of our great God and Savior, Christ Jesus; who gave Himself for us, that He might redeem us from every lawless deed and purify for Himself a people for His own possession, zealous for good deeds.

Let me interject a telltale sign of heresy: a ministry that emphasizes the Lord's return but does not, with equal gusto, emphasize a godly life. Mark it down. Whoever highlights the coming of Christ is also responsible to teach the importance of a pure life. Why not? They mesh together, like teeth in gears. If indeed He is coming again, there is one thing we want to have in place—personal purity.

I wouldn't have much confidence in a person who prides himself in being a good surgeon who at the same time doesn't worry too much about sterile instruments. Wonder how many patients he would have if he said, "To tell you the truth, I've got a new plan in surgery. We do all of our surgery in the back room here at the clinic. I just push this stuff out of the way, then you crawl up on the table, and I'll give you a shot. You've got nothing to worry about."

One thing about practicing good medicine is that you cooperate with the rules of sterilization. You can't be too careful about cleanliness and sterility. And if anyone is going to talk about the coming of the Lord Jesus, then be sure that the same person balances all that talk with an emphasis on purity of life.

The apostle John agrees wholeheartedly with Paul's words to Titus:

> See how great a love the Father has bestowed upon us, that we should be called children of God; and such we are. For this reason the world does not know us, because it did not know Him. Beloved, now we are children of God, and it has not appeared as yet what we shall be. We know that, when He appears, we shall be like Him, because we shall see Him just as He is. And every one who has this hope fixed on Him purifies himself, just as He is pure (1 John 3:1-3).

Why, of course!

We have been to enough splendid, unforgettable weddings to realize that the object of attention is the beautiful bride, dressed in white. The excitement of the entire ceremony occurs when the center aisle doors are opened and the organist begins to play full crescendo, as the bride, with her proud (and often frightened) father, is making her way down to the altar.

Finally, she stands there in all her purity. Although I have officiated at hundreds of wedding ceremonies, I will never get over the thrill of that moment! Did you know that our Lord often calls His church His bride? Like a bride of beauty and purity in no other color than white, all Christians represent that they are pure "spiritual" virgins awaiting the joys and intimacies of heavenly marriage with their Groom. What an analogy! John's words seem so appropriate: "Everyone who has this hope . . . purifies himself."

But how? How can we maintain such a commitment to purity? We learn to live by short accounts. We refuse to let the filth of our life stack up. We don't ignore even the little things that have broken our fellowship with God or with others. We are to live, in the words of the New Testament, with "a conscience void of offense." That's how we can dress in white for His coming, as a bride prepares for her groom.

Perhaps all of that is included in our judging ourselves so that we may not be judged.

Watch

Let's look next at the word *watch*. In the Gospel by Mark, chapter 13, the word *watch* is implied in the commands "Keep on the alert!" and "Stay on the alert!" and "Be on the alert!" Observe those three commands in these seven verses:

> Heaven and earth will pass away, but My words will not pass away. But of that day or hour no one knows, not even the angels in heaven, nor the Son, but the Father alone. Take heed, *keep on the alert*; for you do not know when the appointed time is. It is like a man, away on a journey, who upon leaving his house and putting his slaves in charge, assigning to each one his task, also commanded the doorkeeper to *stay on the alert*. Therefore, *be on the alert*—for you do not know when the master of the house is coming, whether in the evening, at midnight, at cockcrowing, or in the morning—lest he come suddenly and find you asleep. And what I say to you I say to all, *"Be on the alert!"* (vv. 31-37 emphasis mine).

In light of the urgency in Jesus' words, I find it nothing short of remarkable how many days we live without a single conscious thought flashing through our minds regarding Christ's return . . . not even a passing thought. Isn't it amazing? I've noticed that those who become increasingly more sensitive to spiritual things fix more and more of their attention on His coming. And they don't need the reminder from others.

We have all had the same experience of someone's telling us that he's going to come see us on a particular day. He doesn't state a time, but he tells you it'll be sometime during that day. As time wears on through that day, the more often we look. We check the street out front so often that we get the drapes dirty! We're looking. We're watching. We keep waiting until night falls. We turn the front porch light on. We make sure the door is unlocked. We check it four more

times to make sure! Why? Because we're anxiously anticipating our friend's coming. We watch every set of head-
lights that comes around the corner. We stay alert. We are
thinking about it. That's what our Lord has in mind here.

I'll be honest with you. Maintaining a balance in all this is
tough to do. When I teach on prophetic subjects, I feel a little bit like a parent who warns a child against a stranger.
Hoping to guard people from fanaticism, I might go too far
and talk them out of being full of anticipation. Parents who
teach children to be careful about strangers have to be careful not to overdo it. A child can begin to live so suspiciously
that everyone is in question—no one can be trusted. It's
easy for a child to "overlearn" such warnings.

So while I warn you against the extreme of foolish fanaticism, let me quickly add that God honors watching, having a
heart that pumps faster, when we think of His Son's return.
In fact, do you know that there's a reward promised?
There's an actual crown that will be given for people who
live lives full of anticipation of His coming.

> I have fought the good fight, I have finished the course, I
> have kept the faith; in the future there is laid up for me the
> crown of righteousness, which the Lord, the righteous Judge,
> will award to me on that day; and not only to me, but also to
> all who have loved His appearing (2 Tim. 4:7-8).

The "crown of righteousness" is reserved for all who live
their lives anticipating the Savior's return. He honors us for
living with a watchful eye. By the way, it's a whole lot easier
to keep our lives pure when we realize His coming is near.
There's a lot of built-in motivation when we think that His
return will usher in the "Judgment Seat of Christ." That is
why Jesus exhorts us:

> Be dressed in readiness, and keep your lamps alight. . . .
> And be sure of this, that if the head of the house had known
> at what hour the thief was coming, he would not have al-
> lowed his house to be broken into. You too, be ready; for the
> Son of Man is coming at an hour that you do not expect (Luke
> 12:35,39-40).

Worship

In all my years of attending church services and hearing the Bible taught, I cannot remember hearing much said about the importance of worship as we await Christ's coming. But it is clearly an emphasis in Scripture, just as important as occupying, purifying, and watching. I'll write only a little about worship here since I plan to address the subject at length in another book in this study series.

The biblical basis for my comments on worship is found in 1 Corinthians 11:23-26.

> For I received from the Lord that which I also delivered to you, that the Lord Jesus in the night in which He was betrayed took bread; and when He had given thanks, He broke it, and said, "This is My body, which is for you; do this in remembrance of Me." In the same way He took the cup also, after supper, saying, "This cup is the new covenant in My blood; do this, as often as you drink it, in remembrance of Me." For as often as you eat this bread and drink the cup, you proclaim the Lord's death until He comes.

How long are Christians to participate in worship? How long are we to gather around the Lord's table and hold in our hands the elements that symbolize our Savior's body and blood? He tells us in the last three words—"until He comes." Every time we worship around the Lord's table, it is another reminder that He's coming. One of these times will be our last time to observe it on earth. It's kind of exciting, isn't it? It will be our last spiritual meal on earth together. But until then, we are to worship the Lord Christ. Every meal at His table is another reminder that His coming is nearer. We worship Him with great anticipation.

How to Stay Alert and Ready

There's no reason to get complicated about this matter of in-the-meantime living. A couple of thoughts seem worth emphasizing.

The first is: Remember Jesus promised it would occur someday (and He tells the truth!). Keep that in mind. When you read the paper, think of His coming. And remember His promise to return as you see events transpiring that relate to the nation Israel or relate to calamities in our times or those signs and tragedies He predicted would be telltale signs of His arrival. Each of these events—while not directly connected to Christ's return—collectively assure us that we are certainly living in the last days. Call it to mind when you hear of such events, when you lose a loved one, or when something of value is cut out from under you. Hope in the future takes the sting out of the present. Life won't be so hard if we learn to live in the conscious hope of His soon return.

Here's a second tip: Realize the promise could occur today (and that will be the moment of truth). Let me make a suggestion. Let me help you form a new habit for getting out of bed in the morning. Just as soon as your tootsies hit the floor, even before you lift yourself up to your feet, look out the window. As you look, repeat these two lines:

"Good morning, Lord.
Will I see you today?"

I've started doing that and it is amazing how often I have seen Him in my morning or in the face of a child, in a circumstance that I would otherwise have missed Him, in a response from an individual, in an interruption, in a telephone conversation. One of these days, sooner than many of us think, we'll see Him in death. And who knows? One of those days in which we've said those two sentences will be the day He'll come. How great to be able to say, "Why, hello, Lord . . . I've been looking for You."

When former President Eisenhower was vacationing in Denver a number of years ago, his attention was called to an open letter in a local newspaper, which told how six-year-old Paul Haley, dying of incurable cancer, had expressed a wish to see the President of the United States. Spontaneously, in one of those gracious gestures remembered long after a man's most carefully prepared speeches are forgotten, the President decided to grant the boy's request.

So one Sunday morning in August, a big limousine pulled up outside the Haley home and out stepped the President. He walked up to the door and knocked.

Mr. Donald Haley opened the door, wearing blue jeans, an old shirt, and a day's growth of beard. Behind him was his little son, Paul. Their amazement at finding President Eisenhower on their doorstep can be imagined.

"Paul," said the President to the little boy, "I understand you want to see me. Glad to see you." Then he shook hands with the six-year-old, and took him out to see the presidential limousine, shook hands again and left.

The Haleys and their neighbors, and a lot of other people, will probably talk about this kind and thoughtful deed of a busy President for a long time to come. Only one person was not entirely happy about it—that was Mr. Haley. He can never forget how he was dressed when he opened the door. "Those jeans, the old shirt, the unshaven face—what a way to meet the President of the United States," he said.[1]

I can tell you a situation that could be a lot more embarrassing than that. One day there will be a shout, a voice, a trumpet blast, and we won't even have *time* to change clothes. Instantly, we'll be swept into His glorious, eternal presence.

But . . . until He comes, what? Remember the watchwords: occupy, purify, watch, and worship. If you're engaged in those four things, you won't have to get ready, you'll *be* ready! No need to set a date or quit your job or dress in white. Just live every day as if this were the one.

"At the appointed time, the end shall be." One of these days will be "the appointed time." You are ready, aren't you?

Extending Your Roots

Write the four "watchwords" in the front of your Bible or—better still—at the beginning page of each new month if you use a date book or calendar— OCCUPY, PURIFY,

WATCH, WORSHIP. To cement these concepts in your mind, explain to someone else the life-impact of each of these words.

Jesus will appear "at the appointed time." One of these days will be that time. For one week, use the following chart to see how all hours of each day are spent.

Sunday

Monday

Tuesday

Wednesday

Thursday

Friday

Saturday

1. At the end of the week, use these questions to help evaluate your time.

• Where did you spend the most time?
• How much daily time did you spend in prayer and Bible study?
• How often were you involved "at the church"?
• How much time was spent with family?
• How many total hours were spent in recreation, vocation, shopping?
• How many hours were spent doing nothing?

2. The Lord's return should be a time of joy. Are there any changes in your life-style that need to be made in preparation for His return?

But . . . in the Meantime

1. Think seriously about these Scripture passages:
   Matthew 24:36-51

Mark 13:32-37

Luke 21:34-38

Notes

Part I

Chapter 1

1. Joan Welsh, *Quote Unquote,* ed. Lloyd Cory (Wheaton Ill.: Victor Books, 1977), 81.

2. Arnold Toynbee, "Traditional Attitudes Towards Death," *Man's Concern With Death*, ed. Arnold Toynbee, et al. (New York: McGraw-Hill, 1968), 63.

3. Peter Marshall, *John Doe, Disciple: Sermons for the Young in Spirit,* ed. Catherine Marshall (New York McGraw-Hill, 1963), 219-20.

Chapter 3

1. Jon E. Braun, *Whatever Happened to Hell?* (Nashville: Thomas Nelson, 1977), 11-12.

Chapter 5

1. J. Kerby Anderson, *Life, Death, and Beyond* (Grand Rapids, Mich.: Zondervan, 1980), 81-82.

2. A paraphrase of the composite experience describe by Raymond Moody, Jr., M.D., *Life After Life* (New York: Bantam Books, 1975), 21-23.

3. Anderson, 110.

Part II

Chapter 10

1. C. S. Lewis, *Mere Christianity* (New York: Macmillan Co., 1958), 104.

Chapter 15

1. J. Dwight Pentecost, *Prophecy for Today* (Grand Rapids, Mich.: Zondervan, 1961), 19.

2. H. L. Turner, "It May Be At Morn."

Chapter 16

1. Billy Graham, *World Aflame* (Garden City, N.Y.: Doubleday, 1965), 206-7.